Sexuality and the Catholic Priesthood

Based on interviews with Roman Catholic seminarians, priests and former priests, as well as with managers of seminaries, teaching staff, psychologists and psychiatrists, this book considers the lives of the clergy, beginning with the period before entering the seminary. With attention to both heterosexual and homosexual relationships – and so addressing the tension that exists between Catholic teaching and the reality of clerical lives – this wide-ranging description of seminary life encompasses many issues which are not strictly sexual or emotional, such as time organisation, the importance of study, hierarchical relations and friendship. Showing that the lives of seminarians – and later, priests – are absorbed in balancing the expectations of their role with their need for an emotional life and with maintaining an independent, free inner self, with the result that celibacy can come to be viewed as a pretence to be upheld scrupulously in the public sphere only, *Sexuality and the Catholic Priesthood: The 'Chaste' Caste* will appeal to scholars of sociology and religious studies with interests in gender and sexuality, the Catholic Church and priestly vocations.

Marco Marzano is Full Professor of Sociology at the University of Bergamo, Italy.

Routledge Studies in the Sociology of Religion

A platform for the latest scholarly research in the sociology of religion, this series welcomes both theoretical and empirical studies that pay close attention to religion in social context. It publishes work that explores the ways in which religions adapt or react to social change and how spirituality lends meaning to people's lives and shapes individual, collective and national identities.

Society and the Death of God
Sal Restivo

The Transformation of Religious Orders in Central and Eastern Europe:
Sociological Insights
Stefania Palmisano, Isabelle Jonveaux, Marcin Jewdokimow

Bisexuality, Religion and Spirituality:
Critical Perspectives
Andrew Kam-Tuck Yip, Alex Toft

Contemporary Monastic Economy
A Sociological Perspective Across Continents
Isabelle Jonveaux

In Defence of Married Priesthood:
A Sociological Investigation of Catholic Clerical Celibacy
Vivencio Ballano

Beyond New Atheism and Theism
A Sociology of Science, Secularism, and Religiosity
Sal Restivo

Sexuality and the Catholic Priesthood
The 'Chaste' Caste
Marco Marzano

Sexuality and the Catholic Priesthood
The 'Chaste' Caste

Marco Marzano

LONDON AND NEW YORK

Cover image: Philippe Lissac / Getty Images

First published 2025
by Routledge
4 Park Square, Milton Park, Abingdon, Oxon OX14 4RN

and by Routledge
605 Third Avenue, New York, NY 10158

Routledge is an imprint of the Taylor & Francis Group, an informa business

© 2025 Marco Marzano

The right of Marco Marzano to be identified as author of this work has been asserted in accordance with sections 77 and 78 of the Copyright, Designs and Patents Act 1988.

All rights reserved. No part of this book may be reprinted or reproduced or utilised in any form or by any electronic, mechanical, or other means, now known or hereafter invented, including photocopying and recording, or in any information storage or retrieval system, without permission in writing from the publishers.

Trademark notice: Product or corporate names may be trademarks or registered trademarks, and are used only for identification and explanation without intent to infringe.

Translated by Isabelle Johnson, the book is a full translation of the original Italian version (La casta dei casti. I preti, il sesso e l'amore) published by Bompiani.

British Library Cataloguing in Publication Data
A catalogue record for this book is available from the British Library

ISBN: 9781032547077 (hbk)
ISBN: 9781032547084 (pbk)
ISBN: 9781003426271 (ebk)

DOI: 10.4324/9781003426271

Typeset in Times New Roman
by Taylor & Francis Books

Contents

Acknowledgements vii

1 The Autobiographical Roots of a Research Project: The Mystery of Clerical Sexuality 1
2 In Search of the Truth: The Story of a Challenging Enquiry 8
3 Catholic Priesthood and Pastoral Power: An Unbreakable Union 14
4 Chastity and Sacrality in Catholicism: The Celibacy of the Catholic Clergy 20
5 Manufacturing 'God's Men': The Task of the Catholic Seminars 27
6 Seminars as Total Institutions 32
7 Personal Identity and Clerical Vocation: Who Goes Into a Seminary Today? 38
8 Obsession and Guilt: Seminarians' Troubled Sex Lives 47
9 Homophobia and Homophilia in the Seminaries: Two Faces of a Single Coin 55
10 Homosexuality in the Seminaries – Pain, Denial and Cynicism 62
11 Rare Birds in the Seminaries: The Challenging Lives of Heterosexual Students 75
12 The Elephant in the Room: Secrets, Denial and Lies in the Training of the Catholic Clergy 82
13 A Free for All: The Sex Lives of Heterosexual Priests 86

14	Emotional Needs and Unbridled Sex: The Homosexual Clergy	94
15	Clerical Lies and Public Welfare	101
	References	107
	Index	111

Acknowledgements

My heartfelt thanks go to all those who read and commented on the first version of this book or made suggestions and potential theoretical insights. I would like to thank Marco Bontempi, Asher Colombo, Enzo Pace, Mimmo Perrotta, Igor Sotgiu and Isacco Turina, in particular. I am also very grateful to Antonio Scurati for believing in this book right from the start, and to Andrea Tramontana for all the patience, kindness and great professionalism he put into drafting and finalising the book, contributing significantly to improving it. Special thanks also go to Giulia Rocchi for her patience, constant encouragement and affection.

1 The Autobiographical Roots of a Research Project

The Mystery of Clerical Sexuality

A question a psychologist friend asked me on a walk in the Bergamo hills kept coming back into my mind. I'd been telling him about the initial progress I'd been making in the research I'll be describing in this book. We were nearly at the top of Colle di San Vigilio hill and he asked me point blank: 'Some time I'd like you to tell me why you're so interested in this subject.' From that moment on I began thinking incessantly about it. What was it that had been making me want to research the Catholic clergy and, above all, matters relating to priests' sexuality and emotional lives for years? I'm not attracted to the positivist legend of the need for scholarly detachment from the subjects enquired into and so I have no difficulty admitting that my interest goes well beyond the simple question of academic importance and derive for the most part from my personal life story.

Answering this question requires me to go back in time to 1974. I was living in Turin, then, the city I was born in. Mine was a cultured lower middle class family background. My father taught maths at high school and my mother had just decided to stay at home to look after my newborn little brother, after over ten years working in the office of a Fiat supplier. My father was an atheist and generally indifferent to the matter of children's education. My mother, on the other hand, had recently become a fervent Catholic. It was precisely this religious rebirth – together with the insistence of an older fellow parishioner with a son my age and, to an even greater extent, the fears of the prevalence of violence and drugs in state schools then so rife amongst the lower middle class in the great northern Italian cities – which induced her to enrol me at the same church-run middle school that her brother had been so unhappy, low-achieving and apathetic at 25 years earlier.

I passed the entrance test, was allowed into the school and, by a cruel twist of fate, put in the same class my uncle had been in all those years ago. I was thus unlucky enough to be taught, for literature, by the very same cruel, vicious teacher who had tortured my uncle in the mid to late 1940s. Father Carlo[1] always wore a long black cassock and sported a shock of greasy jet-black hair full of dandruff mixed up with hair oil and a nasty sneer on his face. He nurtured an overweening and authentic disdain for his fellow human beings and his pupils, who he generally considered to be worthless and

DOI: 10.4324/9781003426271-1

inferior beings. He engaged in psychological torture, obliging us to write to dictation for hours and hours and then checking through our work with a fine tooth comb, insulting us liberally and sometimes, when he'd had enough, moving onto physical brutality in an entirely personal style involving placing his hand on the forehead of his hapless victim and pushing the latter's head violently back against the wall whilst, at the same time, never failing to repeatedly call his victim 'crapone' ('bone head', as in Piedmontese 'crapa' means 'head'). During break he would sidle up to the little gatherings of pupils in the school playground and ask, in a simultaneously intimidating and tongue-in-cheek, derisory manner, what we were talking about, i.e. what the subject of our conversation was. Father Carlo was a cruel man. I defended myself against him for three years by attempting to make myself totally invisible – a 'non-person' – ensuring that I was neither seen nor heard. I think I unconsciously realised, at the time – and it is something I have given further thought to decades on – that the boys who attracted Father Carlo's attention, for both good and ill, were either the very studious and obliging boys, the 'teacher's pets', or those who struggled academically, the boys he called 'craponi'. I certainly didn't want to be thought naughty, given what that meant, but neither did I want to be one of the 'pets', the favourites of this 'black crow', as we boys called him. This aura of mediocrity, the anonymity of the group in the middle, was my primary goal, my elementary survival strategy in what was, for me, a bleak and frightening world. 'Neither joining the club nor rebelling against it': this sums up my approach. The idea of joining the club revolted me, but I wasn't strong enough to rebel against it either, materially or psychologically. Today I can see that what I was doing, even at the time, was adopting an observation vantage point, as the researcher and ethnographer that I was to become: neither insider nor outsider, neither too detached nor too involved.

My rebellions against a system which was so drastically stronger and more violent than I was were then silent ones, frequently made together with other 'prisoners' of that grim institution. During those terrible hours of dictation and handwriting with Father Carlo, my colleagues and I played games such as lifting the chairs of our two-person desks in order to make it look like we were sitting when we weren't, at least for a few seconds. It was a game which required multiple skills: lifting our chairs without being seen, looking as if we were sitting down even if we weren't and, lastly, lowering our chairs again without being noticed and sitting down again. It was an extremely risky and also painful operation, as all those athletes who do the same as they get ready to ski down a slope well know. It was painful but it was, at least this once, self-inflicted pain, independent of the will of our dark tormentor. There is no doubt that Father Carlo subtly enjoyed torturing us but he was very probably not a paedophile. I think he cultivated such a profound hatred for humanity in its entirety as to be incapable of seeking intimacy, even perverse intimacy, with a teenager. His misanthropy was so extreme that the only mass he held was shut up in a deserted chapel on the first floor of the school, always without listeners, or at most one or two fellow priests. I still struggle to imagine such a pure sadist talking of love, divine mercy, forgiveness or grace.

It was a different story with other teachers at the school. Stories circulated in the school of the erotic exploits of some of these with one or other of our schoolmates. Father Mauro's reputation as a paedophile was consolidated, for example, and took the form of a boundless passion for measuring the body temperatures of feverish boys rectally. Stories revolving around fiery Father Carmine, the music teacher, were equally rife. In the classroom he was subject to violent attacks of rage in which he slapped the boys, but in private he was a passionate 'snogger' of pupils whom he dragged in to play the piano on some pathetic excuse. In those three miserable years, during which I lost all vestige of religious belief, I unconsciously – and it is only with hindsight that I have managed to grasp this too – adopted the very same strategy with these probable abusers which had worked so well with Father Carlo: making myself invisible, turning myself into an nondescript, spineless and silent creature, a middle-of-the-road, passive pupil, but never bad enough to be noticed and punished.

I must also admit that I was myself never molested and I do not remember how, from whom and in what circumstances I came to know of Father Mauro and Father Carmine (and at least one other priest, Father Alberico, the details of whose perversions I cannot remember). What I do remember clearly is that the victims of these behaviours were certainly anything but enthusiastic about what had happened to them and we all ardently hoped with all our hearts that we ourselves would never be subject to these 'special attentions' from our teachers. So we were, perhaps, happy that these things were happening to others rather than us and desperately hoped that it would never be our turn. We knew that the risk came from two or three specific sources and that not all priests had this same penchant for sexually abusing teenagers. In any event I am in no doubt as to the truth of these stories. They were anything but figments of our imaginations. Where would we have got the idea from? How could our teenage minds have spawned the thermometer and piano stories (and others) without any basis in truth? Indirectly confirming this is the fact that I spent all my summers in those years at a holiday home run by the same order as the school's and there I neither saw nor heard anything like it. And this despite the opportunities being there, as such holidays involved us living together for many weeks.

Clearly neither at the time, nor for some time afterwards, would I have used the word 'abuse' for the priests' kissing and groping. Like my schoolmates I saw them as unpleasant for those on the receiving end of them but somehow inevitable, essential features of that claustrophobic, closed, authoritarian and entirely male world which very soon disgusted me, prompting me to move away from religion as soon as I could, i.e., in year four at a state high school, and throw myself into the lively anti-establishment atmosphere of the 1970s. I still clearly remember the appeal for me as a boy – I was probably in year three of middle school – of the shouting and slogans coming from the wide tree-lined avenue our windows looked out onto during the public protests. The windows in our 19th century classroom were all rigorously obscured to block out what was happening out there, to stop us being distracted from the everyday torture of our school lives, but the shouts and slogans of the tens of thousands of people on the street below could not be shut out. And very soon this, for me, was freeing music to my ears into whose warm embrace I ardently hoped I would shortly be released.

Over the years I have obviously experienced other forms of oppression but nothing as totalising and violent as my church school years. For the rest of my youth I did everything I could to avoid ending up in situations such as those, opting for conscientious objection to avoid being called up, for example, despite never having been a radical pacifist, in ideological terms.

I can now see that the sexual abuse which I did not label as such at the time was part of a system of fierce teenage discipline which encompassed a number of other forms of harassment too: forced prayer, writing in immaculate handwriting in dictation, the priests' coldness and profound psychological contempt for us, the 'strict' (and never stimulating) curriculum taught to us and physical ill-treatment. It was this framework of total depersonalisation, that stripping away of all our rights, as if we were saplings to be brought up straight trunked with all imaginable punishments, that made the abuse possible – the groping, the thermometer forced up the anus, the old priest's tongue in pupils' mouths. Naturally the discipline and obedience extended beyond the confines of the school, too, into our homes, keeping us quiet about what was going on, stopping us from reporting what we knew to our parents. Perhaps we also feared a slap, of being accused of talking rubbish, of bringing out into the open what adults saw as silliness, childish fantasies, teenage idiocies. I don't think my parents would have taken me seriously if I had told them what I have written here. They would have told me to shut up and get down to my school work. That was what was important to them. This is what they had sent me to that school for, with all the sacrifices this involved, and what they expected in return was gratitude and good school performance, something they did not get in those three dark years, perhaps the worst of my life.

A further factor in those years increased my detachment from religion and priests. My father, the maths teacher, changed school and my home was soon a hive of activity, with frequent visits from many of his new colleagues and their friends, all artists and intellectuals for whom life's bywords were freedom, anti-conformism and systematic defiance of the lower-middle class values which my family had lived by until then. Naturally all this made the school I had to go to even more unbearable and hateful to me. In any event, the motley crew of people who started toing and froing through my home included a priest – an unusual, intelligent, ironic man who rebelled against many of the commonplaces of the day. Father Federico was a significant adult for me and I remained very fond of him for many years, until his death.

There was just one moment of tension between us. It was when, in the summer of 1975 or perhaps 1976, my parents sent me to spend a few days of holiday at the presbytery in his parish, deep in the countryside. His nephew Valerio came with us and a few days later the latter sent me to visit what he called the 'treasure', i.e. his uncle the priest's huge collection of pornographic magazines kept in an old cupboard next to his bed. It was then that I discovered illustrated and narrated sex. A few days later some of these magazines were found under our mattresses – where Valerio and I had hidden them – by the housekeeper and we were reported to the priest who shouted at us and threatened to send us home. So once again, an encounter with a priest was associated with eros. And concealment, prohibition and repression.

To my great joy I left the Catholic middle school in 1977 to join a state high school. Two years later, at the age of fifteen, I met Father Pietro, my religious education teacher. Father Pietro was an erudite, intelligent man but also an extremely ugly one. He was physically repugnant, fat, frequently smelly, wore filthy clothes and sported a long unkempt beard, in orthodox pope style, which was full of food and saliva. He was right wing, a fierce traditionalist and a die-hard conservative. This meant that with me – now an entirely atheist militant communist – he frequently got into heated verbal combat. His lessons frequently culminated in duels between the two of us, constant cut and thrust, which was certainly a great dialectical training ground for me, preparing me to do battle with the 'enemy'. Father Pietro was soon enjoying his discussions with me so much that he started insistently if subtly inviting me to his home. He used to say: 'one Saturday after school come to my home, we'll have a bite to eat and I'll show you my books. We'll finally be able to chat without watching the clock on the subjects we both love.' In the end I gave in but on condition that he also invited a schoolmate of mine so that I would not be alone with him. Something told me that I should watch my back. I remember perfectly everything about that day: his wonderful home in the city centre, its grand circular entrance giving access to at least six rooms, the huge number of books this rich man owned, the frugal meal consisting of little more than a salad eaten together in his very large dining room. After lunch Father Pietro encouraged me and my friend to sit down on a three seater sofa. 'For a nap', he said. When we had sat down he joined us, with me in on the middle cushion, and spread a woollen blanket over our knees. Then he closed his eyes but he certainly wasn't sleeping because his right hand began moving in the direction of my thigh, which he gently caressed, and then began moving upwards. I managed to stave off the attack a few times by edging over to the other side of the sofa, towards my friend. At the third attempt I got up and said that unfortunately we had to go. It was getting late and my parents were expecting me. What amazes me now if I think of this episode is that I said nothing about it to anyone: not my mother or father, not my schoolmates (perhaps with the exception of the boy who went with me that day, but only briefly, in the heat of the moment and immediately afterwards), not to anyone else. It's difficult to understand: I – communist, atheist, heterosexual – continued to spend time with this vile, disgusting priest as if nothing had happened, as if I had never felt that hand on my thigh creeping upwards in search of the private parts of a 15-year-old extremely innocent virgin. Father Pietro and I continued to discuss and argue right through my high school years, until I left. It was only much later, I would say fairly recently, that I fully grasped the seriousness of what might have happened if I had not been so quick to react or perhaps just more in awe of that priest. If I think about it now, on the strength of what I now know from a great many stories of clerical abuse of teenagers, I am aware that in actual fact I was ashamed of what happened and that with Father Pietro I had broken the rule I had internalised at middle school just a short time earlier, on the importance of invisibility and anonymity. During his lessons I had drawn too much attention to myself and made myself an object of his desire, an attractive sexual object. And I had done so, in all likelihood, because I felt stronger then than I had at middle school. I was older, openly atheist, communist and interested in girls. And it was a state school. I felt safe. Now I can see that I was not strong enough to report what happened to my mother and the headmaster and that my not doing so meant that the same thing or worse would happen to many other teenagers.

From my university years onwards and right up until a decade or so ago I spent no time at all in any Catholic contexts and set foot in church only for baptisms, funerals and the like. Quite suddenly, however, in 2007, I decided, for research purposes, to buy an organised trip to Medjugorje and from then on I spent a considerable amount of time in parish settings for scientific purposes. It was on one of these 'ethnographic trips' with followers of an evangelising organisation called Rinnovamento nello Spirito that I met a priest I remember almost nothing about, except that he was with a community of followers from Central Italy and that as we were talking he, too, put his hand on my thigh and nonchalantly began massaging it. I moved away immediately and this time I did not keep quiet. I described the episode – one that immediately conjured up my earlier abuse – in detail in my book *Cattolicesimo Magico* (Marzano 2009), telling the whole story of that experience, which was so shocking in various ways.

A few years after the publication of that book I travelled to the United States for a period of research and study. A Catholic friend put me in touch with a little monastery near a large and important university in which the monks were offering to rent me a tiny room for a sum which was little more than symbolic. I accepted happily and met a priest – I think he was Australian – that first evening. He was staying in a spacious flat next to my cubbyhole and right away invited me to dinner. He seemed personable and cheerful. At dinner, on a terrace overlooking the bay, he started talking about the challenges of his vocation, and two glasses of wine later his hand began moving up my thighs, entirely unembarrassedly. I left right away and avoided him entirely for the rest of my stay. The arrogance in what he did still comes to mind: the brazenness of it, the feeling of impunity he must have had – as I was a stranger – the absence of caution. What we are talking about here, what is wrong about this, is obviously not the homosexuality. I have a great many gay colleagues, friends and colleagues, none of whom have ever done anything like this to me. It is the action of someone wanting sex right away, no time wasted.

This book is the direct outcome of the stories I have told here, of the profound desire they prompted in me to understand the nature of the bond between sex and clerical training, to understand the motives behind the clergy's public disinterest and private obsession with sex, to throw light on whether sexuality might potentially be one of the keys to understanding the nature of the thousands-of-years-old institution which has carefully forged and moulded them. The rest of this book recounts what I found out.

Note

1 The names of the people cited in this book are all fictitious, unlike the facts described.

2 In Search of the Truth
The Story of a Challenging Enquiry

Grafted onto the autobiographical roots outlined above, my empirical sociology research into the clergy began some time ago, in around 2009, when I began to spend time in parishes and churches for the purposes of the research which culminated in *Quel che resta dei cattolici* (*What Is Left of Catholics*, Marzano 2012). The theme of priests' sexuality and emotional lives captured my attention almost right away: the dozens of priests I met in these years, in fact, were extremely willing to speak to me about all the difficulties then facing their parishes and themselves personally, as pastors and men of the church, blaming these on the behaviour of certain of their parishioners described as interfering or arrogant and sometimes even going as far as to criticise their bishops to me. But not a single word on their private lives, attitudes to sex and love, sexual preferences or personal troubles escaped them. The more chatty and personable of these men simply glossed over the subject, saying that they had no intention of speaking to me about their private lives, but in the face of personal questions the majority portrayed themselves as martyrs and claimed to have definitively and stoically renounced sex and love and that this mortification of the flesh could now be said to have been accomplished, a job done. This refusal to speak was so absolute, in both groups, that I never had the courage in those early interviews to insist on going deeper, to cast doubt on the truthfulness of these assertions. There would have been no point in any case. I quickly realised that getting to the truth of the matter would require a different approach.

In any event all this got me thinking and curious to the extent that, as a footnote to enquiries relating essentially to the parishes and ecclesiastical movements, I began trying to find out more. I met a Roman woman who had set up an association for women in relationships with priests, both past and present. I interviewed her and was allowed to contact the association's members, who I then travelled all over Italy to interview. It was on the strength of their stories that I began to get a glimpse into the large numbers of clergy with active sex lives, which were consistently covert and frequently troubled and unhappy. I realised that these stories all had a great deal in common and had taken similar paths. The starting point was the woman's attraction to the priest, her admiration for his culture and sensitivity. On

DOI: 10.4324/9781003426271-2

their side the priests grasped the potential in the situation and initiated a subtle and discreet seduction under the cover of friendship. Then came love, true carnal love, initially leading to happiness and then inevitably tormented and painful, above all because the priests – having initially promised to leave the priesthood but claiming to need a little time to muster up the courage to make the break – became more and more evasive, making excuses to avoid meeting the women, and cagey on the subject of building a life with them. Lastly, tragedy struck in the form of the priests' transfer elsewhere, countless unanswered telephone calls, and the priests openly running away and explaining their actions – in the best case scenarios and when an explanation was forthcoming – by a dramatic spiritual crisis, a revival of religious vocations, an unbearable sense of guilt for their betrayal of Christ and his church.

After these 'priests' women' my next step was contacting and interviewing those who had left the ranks of the clergy, former priests, using all available channels. Listening to these stories gave me a deeper understanding of the suffering caused by celibacy, the torment which led thousands of people to shed their cassocks and embark on new lives, marrying, having children and starting new 'normal' careers. For the most part these former priests are people brave enough to give up the perks of clerical life in the name of a more straightforward existence less marked by hypocrisy and double standards. Their leaving the priesthood was not always a conscious decision, however, resulting from an intentional clean break with the past. It was sometimes circumstances – such as a pregnancy – which obliged them to shed their cassocks and take up civilian life, sometimes hurriedly. Many of these men remained at length – perhaps for the rest of their lives – 'accidental laymen' whose identities, mindsets and deeply rooted attitudes acquired during their youth and clerical lives remained with them, either consciously or otherwise. A subtle but persistent nostalgia for their period of celibacy and the priesthood never leaves this type of former priest, even when they are respectable father figures. Ultimately, for this subgroup within the multitude of former priests, leaving the clergy is experienced above all as a failure, the unhappy outcome of a shortcoming, of the inability to experience sexuality and emotional lives, perhaps even fatherhood, while continuing to wear a cassock. This corroborates some of the conclusions I will come to at the end of the book, on the subject of the nature and strength of the bond between the Catholic Church and those working for it.

My first contact with the world of the homosexuality clergy also dates to ten years ago when I interviewed a young bank clerk introduced to me by a young colleague who told me of his long and troubled love story with a gay priest who had decided to come out into the open and leave the church.

Lastly, in those same years I also heard, in first person, the incredible story of the daughter of an African priest and was given the chance to cast an initial glance on priests' attitudes to sexual love on the continent in which Catholicism and the number of priests is growing exponentially.

Overall I gathered a great deal of material and interviewed no fewer than 15 people, but did not succeed in developing a coherent scientific project for it. Ultimately I did not use it. But I never gave up the idea of extending my research and writing a book on the subject and it remained in the background of my 'sociological imagination'. In the meantime, over the intervening years, I continued to work on various aspects of Catholicism and thus acquired a more in-depth knowledge of the clerical world, increasing my contacts within it hugely and adding to my network of these. The definitive input behind my decision to embark on a research project hinging on the Catholic clergy and the issue of sexuality and emotional lives within it, was certain scandals bound up with abuse committed by members of the clergy, such as the Regensburg Cathedral choir scandal in Germany, in 2017, and the scandal resulting from the publication of a report on sexual crimes of the Catholic clergy in Pennsylvania a few months later.

The debate revolving around this, above all in Italy, focused on the subject of the protection given to abusive priests by their bishops and the Vatican. The common theme running through most interpretations of clerical abuse has generally approximated to the following: there are dangerous sexual perverts, 'rotten apples', lurking within the church for some unknown reason, whose crimes are frequently covered up by their superiors (the bishops) wanting above all to avoid scandals with the potential to jeopardise the Catholic Church's good name and reputation. I believe that this is an overly simplistic reading which ultimately trivialises clerical abuse, a reading which presents the problem as something which could be resolved simply by the Catholic hierarchy deciding to deal more harshly with its guilty minions. This explanation struck me right away as highly superficial and entirely insufficient.

In any case, when I began taking an interest in the matter, my interviews with former priests and their partners of ten years earlier immediately came back into my mind. I thus began wondering whether the violence and abuse committed by Catholic clergy was not somehow bound up with clerical education in the seminaries, with the approach to sexuality and the emotions during and after the seminary years. I thus asked myself whether the constant 'covering up' of abusive priests is not an expression of the same organisational culture which has indirectly fostered the abuse itself. The purpose of my research thus soon became casting light on the structural, psychological and cultural elements which explain the sexual crimes committed by priests amongst other things. This focus on the 'system' is obviously not a matter of eliminating or even diminishing the responsibility of the individuals involved – which remains extremely significant in criminal law, and also moral, terms – but rather of highlighting the 'organisational guilt' alongside the individual responsibility, of elements of clerical system functioning which contribute, in certain circumstances, to generating abuse (Catino 2023). To this end, and for the purposes of understanding who the Catholic clergy are, how they are trained and how they deal with their existential difficulties, I thus first examined the international scientific debate on the subject and then contacted and interviewed current and former priests – this time armed with a series of hypotheses and a highly structured series of questions. These priests had to be willing to talk about their lives (their clerical lives but especially aspects relating to their emotional and sexual lives) honestly and I gave them the utmost guarantees of confidentiality. I acquired these contacts in the widest possible variety of ways: some of them were people I had met during earlier research and made fresh contact with; others were contacts passed on to me by friends and acquaintances or other interviewees; in a very few other cases contact was the result of appeals for research participants posted online. Many of the resulting interviews are extraordinary documents that, as you will see, encompass extremely intimate details, events, states of mind, situations, thoughts and experiences which had been set aside for years, sometimes decades, in some silent recess of the memory. I will always be grateful to these interviewees for bringing these to the surface, a process which was taxing and painful for many former priests and certainly risky for the acting priests who trusted my promise not to reveal their identities to anyone. There were forty-one interviews in total, only two of which were telephone rather than face-to-face interviews. They were all (including the phone interviews) rigorously recorded, across the whole country – from Lake Maggiore to Messina – wherever someone was ready to tell me their story. This material was supplemented by ten dialogues with former priests made a decade ago and a similar number of interviews with women who had had relationships with priests. I would like to make clear that, in reporting the contents of the conversations, I have always attempted to make identifying the people concerned impossible. To this end names, places and circumstances have been made generic and unrecognisable or have been replaced with invented names, without otherwise changing the substance of the facts spoken of in any way whatsoever. Once again for the purposes of safeguarding the confidentiality and privacy of the information gathered and avoiding harming anyone in any way, I also decided not to distinguish between the testimony of current and former priests in my presentation of them.

The participation of two former seminary trainers and a grand total of five psychologists (one of whom was a priest) who advised and worked at a range of seminaries added huge value to the research. My long stay (two weeks) at a care home for 'priests in difficulty on psychological or spiritual grounds' in southern Italy was also hugely helpful, above all for the many interviews made with priests, psychologists and staff.

Lastly, a few years ago, I came across Francesco Mangiacapra's incredible 'gay priests dossier', an extraordinary 'natural document' archive (i.e. documents not collected for research purposes) on the sexual behaviours of a few dozen young southern Italian priests, a mine of spontaneous and entirely unfiltered information on the 'private world' of the homosexual clergy.

This is an account of the project's successes – the great deal of data accumulated – in two years of extremely intense work. I cannot, however, conceal the fact that it was the most difficult and challenging sociological research of my no-longer brief professional life. In the past and as a scholar I have ventured many times onto extremely delicate social terrain, such as the communication of terminal illness diagnoses (Marzano 2004) and the peculiar rites of Catholic sects (Marzano 2009, 2012), but I have never faced so many difficulties – so many dead ends, doors slammed in my face, emails not replied to, contacts which came to nothing, so much stubborn refusal to meet me – as I faced during this research. The people who did not facilitate this research or work with me in any way were many and varied: psychologists, priests and Vatican staff. I bear no grudges against anyone for all these 'noes' but I believe that this attitude to a scholar attempting to cast light in an objective manner on significant social phenomena reveals the existence of a specific will by many in the institution to avoid a frank and open public debate on these themes. I suspect that this constitutes yet another expression of the 'culture of secrecy' (Simmel 1906, Morrison and Milliken 2000, Cohen 2013, Cozzens 2004, Zerubavel 2006) which I will describe in detail in this book and which pervades the workings of the Catholic Church to such an extent as to be fully emblematic of it.

The clergy's sexual and emotional lives are the great secrets of the church, taboos which the institution wants to avoid light being thrown on. The implicit belief of many members of the clergy is that disclosing the truth would lead to a collapse in the church's institutional reputation and undermine much of its authority and prestige and this is, in fact, extremely likely.

I will make three concluding observations. The first of these is the scientific approach adopted in this work, which is completely and radically sociological. This means that issues relating to other spheres, such as psychology, history or theology, are touched on only in passing and only as regards aspects truly relevant to a research approach which favours a socio-organisational analysis highly sensitive to themes of power and the motives for social action (Clegg, Courpasson and Phillips 2006, Lukes 2021). All the research work which culminated in this book was ethnographic in nature. The narrative texts which scholars gather during their ethnographic work supply a wealth of structured material which is ideal for organisational analysis above all in cases in which the sociologists gathering them have a high overall knowledge of the worlds described deriving from intense and prolonged contact. It is this background knowledge, together with the size of the documentation deriving from empirical analysis, which guarantees the professionalism and interpretational quality of the work. In this specific case, in-depth interview was the only alternative, given the extreme delicacy of the subject and the need for detailed (Geertz 1973) and complex descriptions of the institutional milieux analysed. Lastly, unlike journalistic analysis, the narrative material deriving from the more than 40 interviews made was analysed with the help, where possible, of comparison with similar research done elsewhere in the world (the triangulation method) and, in any event, the interpretational key supplied by theories and concepts of an inherently sociological type.

Secondly, as regards the specific context of work limited to the seminary training, sexuality and emotional spheres, I deliberately left out of my analysis many other elements in clerical life which are of great importance in understanding the clergy of our day but, I believe, of secondary importance in understanding the underlying ecclesiastical institution–functionary relationship.[1]

My final consideration is a strictly ethical one: my research has no political goals. There is no underlying reform agenda for the thousands-of-years-old Catholic Church. The point is that the lies revolving around the life of the Catholic clergy are no longer sustainable or culturally acceptable. Truth and transparency are now necessities in the public debate around the Catholic Church and its future. On a personal level, with the by no means to be taken for granted support of the director of this book series and its editor, mine is an attempt to contribute to this difficult but necessary task with the sociological rigour so rarely applied to this delicate field of study, free of prejudice but also without feeling overawed by this historic institution. In this I have attempted simply to be frank, to devote myself to intellectual honesty and to the task of revealing an uncomfortable truth to those with no intention of listening to it (Foucault 2010, 2011).

Note

1 A great deal has been written in recent years about the Catholic priesthood's difficulties and crisis in the wake of the social changes triggered by the secularisation of society. For an overview of the subject I recommend work by Dalla Zuanna and Ronzoni (2003), Ronzoni (2008), Castegnaro (2006, 2010 and 2017), Badaracchi (2009), Crea and Mastrofini (2010), Crea (2015), Frings (2018) and Semeraro (2018) among others. I have also written on the subject myself in *Quel che resta dei cattolici* (Marzano, 2012).

3 Catholic Priesthood and Pastoral Power
An Unbreakable Union

American sociologist Arthur Stinchcombe (2000), founder of the population ecology approach, argued that, as a result of what he called an 'imprinting' effect, rather than change organisations tend to retain their original structure over time, for decades or even centuries. These structural forms in turn depend on the social control and power systems available to them in the era of their birth. This explains why organisations working in diverse fields but which emerged at the same time tend to have features in common and function in broadly similar ways.

The main reasons for this 'organisational inertia' (Hannan and Freeman 1984, 1989) are bound up with the huge psychological, cognitive, economic, cultural and ideological costs of change and the considerable benefits of stability and continuity. Over the years, functioning institutions on one hand accumulate organisational know-how – habits which enable them to perform their tasks simply, clearly and repetitively – and, on the other, acquire internal and external social legitimacy.

In the language of another important organisational sociologist, Philip Selznick (2011), over time organisational forms are 'institutionalised', becoming increasingly rigid and static, with the end result being that they acquire an importance in their own right, in cultural and political, but also emotional, terms which significantly exceeds their purely instrumental value as a means to an end. For example, in the case of the seminaries, clerical training could certainly be done differently but traditions are reassuring because they confer a sense of identity, stability and continuity with the past and hugely diminish the stress bound up with the new, with innovation and change. For all these reasons, changing the institutions without destroying them, reforming them incrementally while keeping them alive, is a highly complex and, in fact, virtually impossible task. It is easier to demolish them and build new ones in their place, but this is only feasible when they are hit by crises so severe that they sweep them away, or such as to trigger radical change (Marzano 2018). Obviously some things have changed in the seminaries over time. The institutions set up by the Council of Trent and the Catholic Counter Reformation to hone clerical education and equip it for the challenging times caused by the Church's loss of religious hegemony

DOI: 10.4324/9781003426271-3

and the dissemination of Protestantism in Europe are different in many ways from those of the 17th century. For example, in Western Europe, numbers of minor seminaries have diminished considerably without disappearing altogether. These are designed to take in boys waiting to embark on the full-blown philosophical and theological education which begins after high school and their coming of age and leads to the priesthood. The use of space has changed, too, with dormitories having disappeared, at least in the major seminaries, and given way to single rooms. Contact with the outside world has increased marginally: seminarians can spend at least one day a week at the family home, as well as their summer holidays, go out of the seminaries more easily and overall have more frequent and intense relations with the outside world than was once the case. Curricula – the body of knowledge passed on to future priests – have also been modified and updated.

These and other things have been modified, with some changes being more important than others. The original imprinting, though, is still clearly visible as the structure underlying the seminaries; their essential form has remained untouched, even after the Vatican II Council. This is because the purpose served by the seminaries is the same. It is still here that the transformation of those 'called by God' from ordinary human beings to 'holy men' devoted to the ultra-special mission of mediating between ordinary mortals, the mass of believers, and God, is presumed to take place. As the Catechism of the Catholic Church[1] reads, in point 1592:

> The ministerial priesthood differs in essence from the common priesthood of the faithful because it confers a sacred power for the service of the faithful. The ordained ministers exercise their service for the People of God by teaching (munus docendi), divine worship (munus liturgicum) and pastoral governance (munus regendi).

Thus, as is well known, in the Catholic Church's symbolic and power universe, priests' status is very different from that of ordinary believers: priests give communion, take confession, absolve sinners and guide, warn and educate their flocks, and it is assumed that their teachings and very special wisdom are indispensable. In Lüdecke's concise terms (2010, p. 475) 'ordination equates priests to Christ in such an incomparable way that they alone can teach, guide religious practice and lead God's people, as "mediators between God and man"'. It is especially via the Holy Communion that the hierarchical system of the division of roles is ritually replicated and internalised: '[...] Praise of God and hierarchical affirmation go hand in hand and are designed to stabilise laymen's existence based on yeses and amens' (Lüdecke 2010, p. 475).

In other words, amongst Catholics the priesthood is not, at least sociologically speaking, universal and shared by all believers but the preserve of an ecclesiastical caste of celibate men who jealously guard their prerogatives.

It is precisely the priestly class institution that makes the Catholic Church, for Weber (1978), the supreme example of bureaucratisation, as all the hierocratic mechanisms associated with charismatic powers previously considered to emanate from exceptional personal qualities have been transferred to a single 'office', a 'post', the priesthood.

The hierarchical principle applies across the board, without exception: functionaries' responsibilities are always and exclusively upwards, to the apex, never downwards to its base, as is true of organisations governed by democratic representation principles. Parish priests have exclusive decision-making powers over everything that happens in the parish (from mass times to the distribution of duties, feast days and church layout) and the role of the pastoral and economic affairs councils is purely advisory, a matter of assistance and loyal support. The bishop has sole power to confirm a priest's posting or transfer him to another parish and the pope has this same exclusive power over the bishops. Once again, choosing the supreme leader is the exclusive preserve of Cardinal Electors, all priests, effectively a few dozen people[2] in an organisation[3] numbering more than 1,000,300,000 baptised Catholics worldwide.

As Max Weber wrote in *Economy and Society* (1978, p. 960) 'Typically, the bureaucratic official is appointed by a superior authority. An official elected by the governed is no longer a purely bureaucratic figure'. The only form of democratisation compatible with the pure type of bureaucratic organisation, argued Weber (1978), is the equality before the law of the dominated, with the latter being all equally subject to autocratic power. The Catholic Church is the perfect embodiment of this principle, despite hesitant innovations introduced in the wake of the Vatican II Council: all laypeople are equally subordinate to clerical authority. In Lüdecke's succinct expression (2010, p. 474) 'The Church minus lay people? Possible. Minus priests? Impossible.' Specifically,

> parishioners are legally required to treat ordained men reverentially, i.e., with great veneration, deference and devotion, in accordance with their spiritual superiority, and to obey them as bearers of jurisdiction with rule breaking behaviour being potentially punishable. Legally speaking, the ordination of the latter is the basis of the subordination of the former.
>
> (Lüdecke 2010, p. 474)

Ultimately the organisation as a whole is a closed, self-referenced system governed by a caste of the elect, the clergy, which tolerates no external interference. In this latter sense the Church as a bureaucratic organisation is much less democratic and open than others, such as the army, for example. The armed forces opened up to women some years ago and are headed, at least in democratic countries such as Italy, by a politically appointed minister of defence and a head of state elected by a representative assembly. In this guise citizens exert some, at least indirect, control and influence over the armed forces, via their representatives. Influence of this kind is unthinkable in the Catholic Church. Its internal organisation reflects its remoteness from modernity, democracy, separation of power practices and the representation principle. These characteristics are undoubtedly a source of institutional strength and cohesion (enabling conflict to be reduced to a minimum and stability and order to be guaranteed at all levels and latitudes), but it is also a source of profound vulnerability as it prevents it from adapting flexibly to external changes.

But what is the nature and raison d'être and what are the foundations of the power claimed and exerted by such an organisation and those of its ministers? The best answer to this question is, I believe, to be found in Michel Foucault's analysis of 'pastoral power'. For Foucault (2007, p. 201) pastoral work consists in the art of 'conducting, directing, leading, guiding, taking in hand and manipulating men'. It is a form of power over people considered by those subjected to it as immensely beneficial and as characterised by a distinctive relationship between the priest (or, in the political context, the sovereign) and God in which the latter can be described as a subordinate pastor 'to whom God has entrusted the flock of men and who, at the end of the day and at the end of his reign, must restore the flock' (Foucault 2007, p. 124). The fruit of pastoral work – what the sheep get out of obeying the shepherd – is first and foremost the salvation promised to all those who acquiesce.

In the pastoral vision characteristic of Catholicism, Foucault continues, salvation can never be achieved alone, i.e. individually. It is always the outcome of accepting the authority of another person, a spiritual director, a guide, a superior, who must be kept informed, above all via the supreme gesture of confession, of all the actions and thoughts of every single member of the flock. The priest can, from time to time and on the strength of his pastoral tools – the conscience analysis techniques learnt during his training years – express his assent or dissent, say that this or that is done this way and we know that it cannot be done otherwise (Foucault 2024, n. p.). The profound nature of the bond explains why each individual member of the flock can only have one shepherd, just as there is only one father and one God. For Foucault a pastor 'teaches truth, teaches writings, teaches morals, teaches God's commandments and the commandments of the Church. In this way he is then a master' (2024, n. p.). Foucault continues:

> The power of the pastor lies precisely in his authority to oblige people to do everything it takes for their salvation: an obligatory salvation […] In a Christian society a pastor is someone who can ask for absolute obedience from others […] The pastor can impose his will on others, and according to his own decision, without there even being general rules or laws, because, and that is what is important in Christianity: people don't obey in order to arrive at a certain result, they don't obey, for instance,

simply to acquire a habit, an aptitude or even a merit. In Christianity, the utmost merit is precisely to be obedient. Obedience must lead to a state of obedience. Remaining obedient is the requisite condition for all other virtues. Obedient with respect to whom? Obedient to the pastor.

(Foucault 2024, n.p.)

In Christianity, Foucault's theory continues, individuals are thus part of a system of generalised obedience which frequently takes the form of the celebrated 'Christian humility', namely a deeply rooted and in some ways internalised tendency to submit to orders from superiors and, through them, to the will of God. The ultimate goal of pastoral discipline is thus eradicating the sheep's will, his or her total submission, and note that this is not to the law but to the person of the pastor, in a bond which Foucault (2007, p. 179) describes as 'complete servitude'. Ultimately from a Christian perspective being humble means an awareness that one's own will is evil and that happiness comes from dependence alone, from allowing oneself to be guided entirely by another person.

The pastorate, constantly reinforced over the centuries and rigidified into a perennial vocation for hierarchy, was born with the Church as an essential attribute of the power exerted over the people by a historically unique organisation which aspires to rule over people 'in daily life on the grounds of leading them to eternal life in another world and to do this not only on the scale of a definite group, of a city or a state, but of the whole of humanity' (Foucault 2007, p. 148).

The whole history of Christian traditions and practices can be read in the light of the affirmation of priestly power.

> What is sacramental power? Of baptism? It is calling the sheep into the flock. And of communion? It is giving spiritual nourishment. Penance is the power of reintegrating those sheep who have left the flock. A power of jurisdiction, it is also the power of the pastor of the shepherd. It is this power of jurisdiction, in fact, that allows the bishop as pastor to expel from the flock those sheep that by disease or scandal are liable to contaminate the whole flock.
>
> (Foucault 2007, p. 153)

Christianity historian Mauro Pesce has effectively summed up the consequences of the political device adopted by what I would call 'Catholic pastoral clericalism' in the following terms:

> A system which divides human relationships into two categories – priests on one hand and laypeople on the other – inevitably adopted a social logic in which priests constitute a social class apart, in sociological terms a managerial class or caste. Set up to form a vertical relationship between people and God, priests inevitably also develop horizontal

relationships between themselves. This naturally generates a social consciousness between priests, a team spirit, which separates them off from other believers. The Church is theoretically laypeople and priests as a whole but in its language and social reality it is, de facto, the priest class alone. The language is revealing: by 'what the Church thinks', 'what the Church does' or simply 'the Church' we mean the priesthood represented by its upper echelons, the priesthood as a whole or individually.

(Pesce 2005, pp. XVI–XVII)

The next chapter will illustrate the bond between pastoral work and celibacy, including the importance of chastity and priestly celibacy to the legitimacy of pastoral power.

Notes

1 https://www.vatican.va/archive/ENG0015/_INDEX.HTM.
2 In June 2024, there were exactly 126 electors, 7 appointed by John Paul II, 27 by Benedict XVI and 92 by Francis.
3 Agenzia FIDES, Agenzia delle pontificie opere missionarie, 2019.

4 Chastity and Sacrality in Catholicism
The Celibacy of the Catholic Clergy

Canon 277 of the Code of Canon Law solemnly declares:[1] 'Clerics are obliged to observe perfect and perpetual continence for the sake of the kingdom of heaven and therefore are bound to celibacy which is a special gift of God by which sacred ministers can adhere more easily to Christ with an undivided heart and are able to dedicate themselves more freely to the service of God and humanity.'

Celibacy and chastity have been mandatory for the whole clergy in the Catholic Church for nearly one thousand years, since the 12th and 13th century[2] Lateran Councils (with the exception of the Eastern rite Catholic Church). To begin to understand its meaning and importance to priests' lives and to the organisation of the Catholic apparatus sociologically (note that its theological implications, and any wider historical analysis of it have been deliberately left out of this work[3]) I will return once again to Weber's *Economy and Society* (Weber 1978, p. 1172). In an important passage regarding the matter at hand here, the great German sociologist wrote that 'the introduction of celibacy [for the Catholic clergy] had represented a reception of monastic forms accepted upon the insistence of the Cluniac movement'. Weber continued, clarifying that the extension of mandatory celibacy from monks alone to the whole clergy around one thousand years ago is to be seen as part of a wider and generalised bureaucratic rationalisation and centralisation process. This extension ultimately meant that diocesan priests resembled monks, i.e. they were 'professionalised', and their lives began to be structured in an ordered and methodical way, in accordance with precise time frames, with all forms of leisure rejected together, in general, with all 'personal obligations that did not serve the purposes of his vocation' (Weber 1978, p. 1173). Lastly Weber (1978, p. 1173) reiterated in his conclusions on this point that 'for centuries the local church authorities (bishops, parish clergy) opposed this overwhelming monastic competition. [...] This struggle of the local authorities was at the same time directed against the bureaucratic centralization of the church.'

Thus in historical competition terms, the monastic celibacy model took precedence over, and decisively outdid, the married lay clergy model in every way, that is spiritually – for the purposes of greater pastoral care-effectiveness including in confessions – ethically, and in terms of teaching and the passing on of faith. In addition to all this there was also undoubtedly an economic factor (relating to the advantages of the absence of family members and heirs as regards the conservation of ecclesiastical assets) frequently cited in historical reconstructions of the genesis of extended celibacy. This latter was certainly an important factor, although it is now decidedly secondary in importance as compared to the factors referred to above, as priests are now all, in Italy at least, paid a salary and thus have incomes and personal assets which do not end up in the Church's coffers when they die or retire.

In any case, priests' celibacy and 'perfect continence' in sexual terms is a formidably effective factor for the Church in at least two ultra-important ways. The first of these relates to the 'total' character of the relationship of trust between functionary and the organisation which celibacy allowed for: for an organisation aspiring to act as an 'ideal bureaucracy' (in Weberian terms) and a 'holy caste', celibate, chaste priests free of family ties and wholeheartedly devoted to their institutional mission was certainly to be preferred, in organisational performance efficiency terms, to married priests with children expecting greater autonomy. The latter group would naturally be less willing to devote themselves wholly to the organisation, less inclined to show absolute deference and subordination towards their hierarchical superiors, the heads of the Church (Wolf 2019). 'Love', wrote former German priest and psychoanalyst Eugen Drewermann, 'is the most dangerous enemy of all totalitarian systems. The best way of judging whether a sociological group is totalitarian or otherwise is precisely this group's attitude to love.'

Furthermore, as another theologian and American priest, Donald Cozzens, has argued (2006, p. 77),

> [...] from an administrative point of view, and here we are talking about power, mandated celibacy is arguably the linchpin of the ecclesiastical system. No one is more controlled than when his or her sexuality is controlled. Control another's sexuality and you control his center of vitality, the core of his identity and integrity.

In some ways, celibate priests remain children for ever, boys who never grow up (Frawley-O'Dea 2007), and precisely for this reason subject to the loving care and paternal solicitude of their superiors (Cozzens 2006). What priests get in exchange for this solemn promise to give up sexuality and affectivity is the chance of a guaranteed lifelong occupation and considerable social respect, a role of prestige and power.

The second of our two perspectives from which mandatory celibacy is functional to organised Catholicism is, however, much more important and pivotal. It is the 'sacred' nature of the institution and its claims to a monopoly on mediation between man and God, definitively, its legitimacy as irreplaceable means of salvation for humanity.

In this sense, celibate, chaste priests enable the organisation to present itself as an 'ideal society' made up of priests, i.e. non-'lay' functionaries, 'special' men, set apart from ordinary people and capable of acting, once again according to Weber, 'sine ira ac studio', motivated by justice and the salvation of others alone, emulating Christ. In many ways, when they enter the priesthood, the clergy enter an ascetic world and are dehumanised, that is they lose many of the faults of human beings, in the eyes of laypeople. What's more, in the popular imagination, they remain aloof from purely irrational affective elements (Weber 1978), ordinary feelings, the love and hate impulses which are normally so characteristic of human behaviour and emotions.

It is sexual abstinence which confirms, beyond a shadow of a doubt, that priests are different from, and superior to, ordinary people. Those capable of controlling their sexual instincts can only belong to a superior race with powers beyond the capabilities of ordinary mortals. This is the decisive and exceptional sign of priests' worthiness of one-of-a-kind consideration and respect, authorising them to exert a pastoral role, guiding and comforting the community as a whole. As Jordan has written (2000, pp. 146–147):

> In popular imagination, and in some clerical self-understanding, nothing is more distinctive of the Catholic clergy than celibacy – not even obedience. Weaknesses in chastity outweighs many other merits and alone constitute grounds for dismissal from formation. I wonder about the converse: How often has 'strength in chastity' been judged solely sufficient for ordination in the presence of many other vices – say, greed or ambition or cruelty.

Jordan hit the nail perfectly on the head here: there are undoubtedly many subtle theological and liturgical distinctions between Catholicism and the rest of Christianity, but these are effectively almost entirely unknown to the lion's share of the faithful. In the eyes of the latter, it is above all celibate and chaste priests and the Roman Pope which mark out the Catholic Church. If these ceased to exist it is likely that most of the Rome Church's institutional legitimacy would follow suit. This is why chastity is so crucial to the qualities sought in aspiring priests. An exception can be made for everything else but sexual imprudence, X-rated scandal and revelations of one's intimate life are cause for instant exclusion from the ranks of the elect. In contrast to duty-packed lay lives priests have just one duty: looking after their 'happily asexual' image.

And the objection frequently made by Catholic reformers to justify change, i.e. the presumed general agreement to 'clerical marriage', makes no difference. Firstly, a majority support the abolition of mandatory celibacy only in certain countries and by no means everywhere in the world. This is what came out of a world survey by Univision in 2014 in ten countries across five continents. In it, majorities of various sizes were in favour of abolition in

France (86%), Spain (73%), Argentina (65%), the US and Brazil (61% and 60% respectively) and Italy and Columbia (57% and 55% respectively), whilst 66% in Mexico, 68% in Congo, 71% in Uganda and 76% in the Philippines were against changes to the celibacy institution. This public opinion gap is even more visible in the results of a survey conducted by the Pew Research Center in 2019 on South American Catholics.[4]

In any event, a considerable part of those in favour of abrogating mandatory celibacy would probably continue all the same to show celibate priests special devotion and respect. In other words, wanting to grant the clergy the chance to marry does not necessarily imply that celibate priests would not be accorded greater and more profound respect. I believe that priests' claims to superior status within the community are based on chastity. Thus there are indeed Catholics who want priests to have family lives like their own but it seems likely that if, one day, their parish priests were truly married and had children they would be less inclined to accept their sole spiritual authority in their parishes.

Returning to the theme of this book, the absolutely pivotal nature of affective and sexual issues in the Catholic clerical order is unsurprising. Sex and love are the only 'primary needs' (Maslow 1970) the Church requires its functionaries to renounce. Future priests are not prevented from eating, drinking, sleeping, walking, talking and so on. Limitations of this sort are limited and circumscribed within the seminaries but no concessions whatsoever are made to the ban on aspiring priests' sexual and affective lives, at least openly. This is the linchpin around which all the Church's attention is focused, its most profound and distinctive characteristic.

Not only is giving up sex for religious reasons – a legacy of the gnostic, Manichean and Neoplatonic traditions – believed to lead to spiritual and philosophical excellence (Cozzens 2006), but it is also the supreme manifestation of the authenticity, purity and immensity of priests' faith, the attenuated equivalent of martyrdom, of extreme fasting and mortification of the flesh, of wearing a hair shirt or a belt of thorns (Kueffler 2011). Only radical and absolute love of Christ can, in the eyes of Catholics, prompt men to give up the pleasures of the flesh, the joys of sex, the desire to have children. It is only those prepared to make the ultimate self-sacrifice for the sake of altruism, virtue and generosity and give up personal gain who are worthy to lead the flock and guide it to the final destination, the pastures of the afterlife (Foucault 2007). In this sense and in the words of many popes, celibate priests are a full-blown eschatological sign, 'angels from heaven', proclaiming and presaging heavenly glory (Wolf 2019, p. 97). In the Catholic cultural configuration their chastity is simultaneously a demonstration of priests' exceptional and extraordinary nature (something ordinary mortals are incapable of) and, by emulating Christ's sacrifice, a way to attract God's benevolence (Weber 1978), the best way of winning His love.

It is important to note that in some extreme and non-mandatory cases, naturally, this vocation for authentic and radical chastity has been taken to the limits, such as Origen, the eunuch saint who castrated himself to put into practice Jesus's commandment to 'make themselves eunuchs for the good of the kingdom of heaven' literally. [...] His self-mutilation was the tangible expression of his theological ideas on the need for reunification of the self with God via the repudiation of carnality and the materialism which sex implies.

(Kueffler 2011, p. 706)

In any event, the Catholic Church's ecclesiastical celibacy norms are now subject to growing tensions in parts of public opinion, above all within the Church, with Catholic reformers calling for its abolition on various grounds (Wolf 2019). From this latter point of view, defending celibacy to the bitter end is perfectly in keeping with the radical resistance to modernity approach adopted by the Catholic Church in the wake of the French Revolution. In opting for identity entrenchment and the exaltation of its difference from the modern world, the Church is staking its claim to ever increasing holiness and purity in a world dominated by sexual freedom. 'The greater the importance of sexual self-realisation for men on earth the purer the Church's ministers must be. The more "marriage for all" becomes modern society's mantra the more the Church presents itself as a virginal community' (Wolf 2019, p. 44).

However, in imposing celibacy on its priests the Church is not simply showing its loyalty to an approach based on total political and cultural rejection of modernity but also defending the superiority of the clerical class and the threat to its right to guide and command the faithful posed by democratic ideas and practices.

In fact, what other means can the Church currently command to demonstrate the exceptional nature, the otherness of its functionaries and the institution as a whole from the people, the flock? This distinction might once have derived from the cultural resources possessed by priests as distinct from the people, from theological notions and parish priests' 'latinorum'. These are resources which are now possessed by a hugely wider pool of people than in the past and for this reason alone they are now unsuited to the task of justifying sacred special status.

So what now marks out the popular image of a Catholic priest from a literature teacher or a psychologist if not his style of life, asceticism and renouncing of a normal love and sex life? More than ever today, all that is left to the Church is to put all its eggs in the sex basket or rather focus entirely on its absence, on the assumption of priests 'ontological diversity' from the rest of God's people. Sexual purity is thus now, more than ever, in recent decades, the tangible demonstration of priests' diversity and the most distinctive and original element in it. There is, perhaps, no need to stress the chain of meanings which leads from all this to the exaltation of ecclesiastical power. It is a short and extremely easy sequence. In the first step the priest is sacred and pure because God has granted him this privilege, because he has been selected by God from amongst other human beings and called to an entirely special life. In the second step the Church is the institution founded by God to nurture, safeguard and foster this sacred purity as a gift of God. In the third and last step the Church is a holy and sacred institution to adore and venerate.

Thus it is via the discipline of celibacy that the Roman clerical bureaucracy takes shape and is incarnated in living, thinking beings, half man and half god, or rather still men but also already gods, beings capable of displaying the essential traits of clerical-bureaucratic action in their living flesh, their exemplary testimony and sacrificial drive, of incorporating and assimilating these into a concrete and universally visible and recognisable form. By means of celibacy priests become living allegories of the Church and its supreme true embodiment. The purity of the sexual lives of each one of them testifies to the purity of the institution as a whole, its separation from, and superiority to, the worldly order, its ability to build special men capable of resisting the most universal and powerful of temptations – sex and love. When they join this 'chaste and pure world' individual priests officially cease to have a life of their own and their individual biographies come to an end. In other words, from the moment in which they give themselves to God or, in sociological terms, to the ecclesiastical institution, they lose all their personal characteristics in the eyes of the flock and become ideal instruments of redemption, asexual pastoral guides with no distractions expending all their energies on leading the community to salvation. Their clerical identity and priestly role occupy every pore of their beings, saturating every particle of their social image.

For many sociologically understandable reasons, then, the Catholic Church has fought tooth and nail in defence of the organisational principle of mandatory ecclesiastical celibacy. Not even a drastic reduction in the priesthood vocation across the developed West and the consequent extreme ageing of the clergy; the reconsideration of Christian marriage by Vatican Council II and the secularisation and immense social change which this brought with it; nor the dissemination of democracy, gender equality and a positive view of marriage for priests have dented the confidence of the Roman Church hierarchy. Nothing has convinced them to date to take the idea of changes to the element which governs the lives of all its functionaries seriously, not even the huge number of scandals which have engulfed local churches the world over. Pope Francis also recently argued against such a change, in his Querida Amazonia apostolic exhortation, in response to arguments by a large majority of participants at the Synod for the Amazon to the effect that the exceptional ordination of married priests would be an answer to a chronic shortage of priests in the remotest parts of the forest. His response sidestepped the matter altogether, confirmed the existing system in its entirety and limited itself to urging bishops to pray for an increase in priesthood vocations and to incentivise the sending of missions to the remotest areas of the Amazon.

The widespread implicit fear is that without mandatory celibacy the distinction between laypeople and clergy would risk disappearing and with it the very foundations on which the Catholic Church has rested since the dawn of its history. What Schoenherr has defined Catholicism's 'techno-structure', its most profound organisational soul, its caste of the elect with a vocation, all this would be jeopardised.

Ultimately celibacy is the linchpin on which the whole system of clerical domination hinges, the firm, resilient nucleus of the whole system's identity. If it went, the whole system would inevitably go with it: seminary training, clericalism, the exceptional nature of the priestly caste. The whole organisation and its 'corporate culture' would be revolutionised and turned on its head. This is a very distant possibility indeed. As Jordan has written (2000, p. 144):

> There where both superficial and deeper changes during the sixties and early seventies. But deep clerical structures were left intact – because the deep logic of mandatory celibacy was left intact. We deceive ourselves if we believe that everything would have been modernised or liberated or redeemed after the council except for the intervention of the counter-revolutionary forces. Priestly institutions are too big, too old, and too carefully constructed to be completely changed in the space of a few years. So the 'conservative' reaction was not a shocking return than a predictable reappearance.

In fact, as a man who knew a great deal about ecclesiastical power, Cardinal and Secretary of State under Pius VI Lazzaro Opizio Pallavicini, said: 'If priests were allowed to marry, the Roman papal hierarchy would be destroyed, the esteem and sublime nature accorded the pope in Rome would be lost.'

Notes

1 See also point 16 of Vatican II Council edict Presbyterorum Ordinis.
2 The relevant norms are Canon 7 of Lateran Council II (1139) and Canon 14 of Lateran Council IV (1215).
3 A great deal has been written on the historical and theological aspects of the issue. Recent work in Italian includes Wolf's well supported work with a large bibliography (2019) and the more balanced and nuanced work of VV.AA. (2008) Petrà (2011) and Semeraro (2018).
4 https://pewrsr.ch/2vkhssF. Here the dividing line is very clear: public opinion in the continent's most populous countries, Brazil, Argentina, Venezuela and Colombia, tends to be sympathetic to the abolition of mandatory celibacy whilst Mexico, Ecuador and Peru show an opposite trend.

5 Manufacturing 'God's Men'
The Task of the Catholic Seminars

There can be no other starting point and general focus for this journey through the clerical world than the place where priests' identities have been forged for four and a half centuries, since the end of the Council of Trent, the seminaries.

This institution is generally spoken of only in relation to the European 'vocational crisis', with almost no mention being made of the fact that there are areas of the world in which seminarian numbers are increasing exponentially and that overall the planet is still today awash with the exclusively male residents of the Catholic seminaries, with a grand total of over 200,000[1] split up almost equally between major (adult theology student) and minor (underage middle school pupil) seminarians. To be precise, there are around 115,000 major seminarians and just over 100,000 minor seminarians.

I have been to seminaries many times and always come away with an impression of them being huge, vaguely spectral places made up of vast empty spaces: long corridors, ultra-high ceilings, quiet footsteps and long silences with huge gardens crossed by praying young people. Everything within them brings to mind places which have lost their people, spaces which have been emptied out and abandoned over time. I got a different impression on just one occasion: it was in the south of Italy and packed with young students. What struck me there was primarily the fact that the only women present were those working in the kitchen or making up the rooms and also that the expressions of many of the young men were too infantile for a twenty-something, that there was something singular and vaguely disquieting in their gazes and way of walking, in their general air. I have also slept at an Italian seminary a couple of times: firstly and for many days during my research work for *Quel che resta dei cattolici* (Marzano 2012) and the second at the end of a lecture in Abruzzo. I lived for three weeks at a 'school of theology' in Cameroon where, by day, the boys studied in the diocesan seminary but the rest of the time they were there. For the duration of my stay I ate together with them and chatted with them and their trainers, observing them in many of their activities. I have also spoken at length about life in the seminaries with all those I met and interviewed for this research project. Above all, I sought information on what it generally concealed, i.e. in

DOI: 10.4324/9781003426271-5

Goffman's (1961) words, 'the underlife of institutions', their most ubiquitous and covert practices.

Before reporting what I have understood of the functioning of the seminars and the training of the clergy I would like to take readers inside the high walls of these institutions with a story, a seminary tale like others which I have told over the years and for this reason extremely representative. It is Carlo's story and I will thus narrate it. Before I begin, however, I would like to warn readers that both this story and many others in this book contain language and facts which may offend the sensibilities of some readers. I regret this, but remaining faithful to the words I heard is crucial to an understanding of the subject of this book.

As soon as he recognised me and realised that I was the sociologist from the north who had come to listen to his story Carlo came up to me smiling. We shook hands warmly and a rapport developed right away. He knew that he would soon be going back in his mind many years, around two decades, to events which might conjure up some still hidden ghosts in some secret nook and cranny of his soul.

I was put in contact with him by a friend who works in corporate training. It all began by chance: during a lesson this friend, for some reason, cited the existential journey of seminarians. At the end of the lesson Carlo came up to him and said point blank: 'You have no idea how familiar I am with seminary life! I was in a seminary! The things I could tell you!' So when I spoke to this friend about my research into 'stories of seminaries and seminarians' this singular and outgoing course member sprang to his mind right away. I begged him to get in touch and ask him to speak to me. So here we were, sitting one opposite the other in the living room of the flat where this man, now a manager, lives with Giulio, his future husband.

Carlo's story began on the day, twenty years ago, in which he attended a 'vocational meeting' in his parish, one of those occasions designed to attract the parish's young people to the priesthood. 'I hoped', he told me, 'that the seminary was a place in which good relationships were built, a place to love the next man and be loved in return.' Carlo was then an 'unusual' teenager, as many told him – hypersensitive, delicate, vulnerable, a boy who liked 'girls' games' as much if not more than 'boys' games'. Even his ultra-Catholic mother had always seen him as especially sensitive. Carlo felt he needed protection, to be sheltered from something terrible, from some monster which lived inside him and was to do with his sexual preferences, with love and desire.

This, then, is how Carlo came to join a minor seminary at the age of fourteen. Once there, he was assigned a spiritual father, in accordance with the norm, a young and fairly troubled priest. He soon became this priest's favourite and Carlo and Father Mario, at least twenty years older than him, began spending a great deal of time together, talking for hours and hours about everything, often stretched out next to one another on the priest's bed. And everyone in the seminary knew about their 'special friendship', prompting considerable jealousy and plenty of malicious gossip among Carlo's companions. Obviously Carlo's superiors were also aware of it but no one was scandalised, no one saw fit to take action. In fact such friendships were by no means rare in Carlo's seminary. Many priests had a favourite. 'Just think', he said smiling,

> that when I decided one day to speak to the rector and asked him, with an ingenuity which amazes me today, whether there was anything bad about thinking of a superior all the time, if it might be the precursor to something wrong or bad, in answer he took my hand and caressed it tenderly. He didn't realise that I was talking about my spiritual father and, thinking I was declaring my love for him, wanted to take advantage!

In any event the Father Mario story ultimately took a dramatic turn. It was an autumn afternoon, immediately after school had started again, and the priest and the fourteen-year-old Carlo were stretched out on the bed together when the former suddenly got up and rushed over to the toilet, at the end of a long corridor in his flat. A few moments later Carlo decided to follow him, afraid that he wasn't feeling well and might need help. When he got to the open door of the bathroom, however, what he saw there was not an adult feeling ill but a man masturbating. When Mario saw Carlo he angrily told him to go away. 'How much pain there was in those words!', Carlo remembers today.

> How much it must have cost him to say that! How much I think he would have wanted me to go into that room instead of leaving. But I was still too innocent to take advantage of that situation. I knew nothing of sex at the time. I didn't know what masturbation was and I hadn't yet realised that I was gay. I only know that the sight disturbed me greatly. That was the end of the Father Mario story. The following year I went to high school and only bumped into him now and again around the seminary.

At high school Carlo also finally fell in love for the first time, one of those great loves which teenagers experience. Of the many interested in him, it was a fellow student in the year above him who won Carlo's heart. It was, for some time, a platonic relationship made up of hundreds of letters and love messages exchanged inside the walls of the seminary, of furtive and innocent cuddles. 'You're making a poofter of me', Silvano told Carlo, his beloved, 'I think of you when I touch myself.' But it was only afterwards, when Carlo was brutally kissed by a further companion who had taken him by surprise one morning in one of the many dark corners of an increasingly deserted seminary, given the drop in vocations, that Silvano's love finally became physical. 'After that guy forced that kiss on me and touched me against my will,' Carlo remembered,

I understood that I wanted to make love gently and that the only person I wanted to do this with was my love Silvano. And finally we did it. It was wonderful. I will always be grateful to him for that, even though it makes me laugh now, thinking of the photo of his wedding that I found online a few months ago. You should see how unhappy he was in that photo, Marco!

At any event, even after making love to Silvano, Carlo was not yet entirely convinced that he was gay. 'I was completely lacking', he calmly admits today,

in tools to understand what was happening inside me. We spoke constantly of love in the seminary but no-one had ever explained the concrete difference between the various forms of love, between loving your mother or a friend and passionate, carnal love. When I was kissed by that violent schoolmate (and after being molested by many others) I went to my spiritual father and told him that I was afraid I was gay and he just told me not to worry, that uncertainties around one's sexual identity were normal at my age and advised me to keep aloof and keep away from the seminary's darker and more isolated corners when I was alone.

In the end the relationship with Silvano came to an end, too, and Carlo was getting angrier and angrier. With a group of his schoolmates he started smoking (and not just cigarettes) secretly, stealing the keys from the priests' refectory to take things from it on a regular basis, stealing school exams from the teachers' staff rooms, climbing over the seminary gates to get out at night, using the rector's moped in the seminary's basement, spying through a secret hole on girls changing to go to the gym nearby with a group of schoolmates. He no longer had the slightest illusions regarding the nature of the seminary by then and observed practices of all sorts including sex trafficking by a group of elderly priests with certain very young foreign children with growing disgust. His homosexuality was more and more clear, even if he forced himself to spend time with the girls he met in the parish during his visits home. The situation got worse when one Sunday in his oratory, he met a former prefect in the seminary, a priest, who he was immediately madly attracted to. They embarked on a relationship but Carlo was terribly jealous and suspected that his partner was involved with other people too. And when his jealousy came out so did his panic attacks and nervous crises. At this point his seminary superiors could no longer ignore what was happening and sent him to a psychologist in an attempt to do something about the situation. 'That woman's goal', says Carlo today,

was to cure me of my homosexuality, cancel out all sexual desire in me, reduce me to an amoeba, "repair" me, making me feel disgusting. I don't want to go into the details of those terrible sessions. All I'll say is that she's dying now and I'm not even a little bit sorry.

In any event at the outset the 'cure' seemed to be working and after a period at home Carlo went back to the seminary and seemed to be calmer. But it was the calm before the storm. When he found out during a trip to London that the young priest he loved was in a more or less settled relationship with a fellow priest, the situation exploded. Carlo threatened to throw himself out of the window; the priest in question reported this to his superiors who removed him from the seminary.

It was to take years of therapy and then meeting Giulio, his loving and serene current partner, for Carlo to feel healed, not of his homosexuality naturally (which is not an illness) but of the tendency to experience it in a guilty and tragic way.

Note

1 The data is that of the FIDES agency, Pontifical Mission Societies, 2019.

6 Seminars as Total Institutions

Grasping the importance of seminaries is a simple matter. They are the places in which humans are to be transformed into superhumans, in which priests – those singular, desexualised, half terrestrial, half celestial creatures – are to be spawned, to serve God and the whole of humanity. It is precisely for this reason that the learning, or rather assimilation, of chastity and detachment from desire and amorous pleasure, in both verbal and corporeal language, in seminarians' rhetoric and proxemics, is the founding purpose behind the whole educational process, the supreme goal on which the organisation as a whole is based. What are seminaries for – as otherwise not especially selective schools – if not to acquire this virtue? Theology could easily be learnt from home whilst leading a normal life. It is chastity and obedience which require a special educational regime.

To achieve their aims the seminaries have adopted all the traits of total institutions (Goffman 1961, Keenan 2012). Their young recruits live segregated lives in closed places, separated off from the rest of the world and peopled by celibate males alone. Communal activities greatly outnumber individual ones and the organisation plans each single moment in the lives of its young internees in the finest detail. From this point of view, too, controlling sexuality is the main goal of the seminary panopticon.

Absolute obedience is expected of seminarians and all interaction with the outside world requires prior permission. 'In the environment of the seminary', wrote Keenan (2012, p. 51)

> compliance and deference are accompanied by lessons in silence and secrecy. What emerges is an unquestioning loyalty towards the institutional Church. Conflict is avoided, and fear of the consequences of speaking out prevailed. If and when individuals showed defiance they received immediate visible punishment.

A strict surveillance system hangs over seminarians' heads, a 'big brother' ultra-attentive to the way seminarians 'talk, walk, dress and speak' (Keenan 2012, p. 41). All forms of critical thought are strictly forbidden.

DOI: 10.4324/9781003426271-6

Here is an example of the inflexible and pervasive organisation imposed in a northern Italian seminary two decades ago, as described to me by Father Franco:

> We got up at six thirty and gathered at seven for prayer (Lauds, meditation or mass). Then we had breakfast together before going to school (with almost all of our teachers being priests) until 12.45. At one o'clock we lunched with a single menu, no choices. After lunch we had an hour's break, spent mainly on games (strictly divided up by class) or a walk. We studied from 2.45 to 4.15 and, after a 30 minute break, from 4.45 to 6.30. Then it was time for vespers or mass. And the rosary. At 7.30 we had dinner with a single menu, no choices. After dinner we had an hour of free time and lastly a few communal cultural activities. At 10 pm another prayer and then off to bed.

'The whole educational system', confided Gianni, a central Italian priest,

> was designed to 'fill up the time', with seminarians being subjects to 'resetting' and 'reprogramming', to use the actual words I heard used by a bishop. Hence the multiplicity of words, everyday homilies, lessons, meetings and disparate initiatives. All this served to 'throw things into' its subjects to educate. Naturally no stock is taken of the real impact of this bombardment on people. What is important for the institutions is that it 'is done'.

'The focus is the lowest common denominator', admitted Valerio, priest and religion teacher in the south of Italy.

> The standard is calibrated not to what is right but to what will work for everyone. It is, for this reason, a very bad education. In most cases the boys leaving the seminary have the same faults as when they came in and perhaps a few extra. Because the tendency is always to put the generic community before individuals. In fact, apart from spiritual guidance and confession, the rest of the educational work is group- and never individual-based.

'The system', a young seminary teacher, priest and theologian explained to me with great lucidity during a long interview, 'is pointlessly punitive'. This punitive focus is the consequence of the total dependence of seminarians on the institution, on the total absence of freedom and individuality and is extremely easy to generate, for example, by cracking down on even the slightest hint of autonomy and critical intelligence. Let me tell you this episode which happened to one of our seminarians: one day the seminary's rector received a letter passing on a report accusing the young man of inappropriate behaviour by a very zealous parishioner, accusing him of 'having a fling' with a local girl, who the boy was accused of taking advantage of his home leave to meet regularly, almost every Sunday. The 'guilty party' was summoned and told that he would not be able to leave the seminary for several months, not even at the weekends. At this point the young man protested his innocence and produced proof that exonerated him entirely: he had never been out with the girl in question and had simply met a group of old friends in the parish he was born and grew up in at the weekends. This proof was definitive and the seminary's superiors were obliged to absolve him of all guilt. 'But we're going to punish you all the same', they added. And when the boy expressed his shock and asked why, they continued: 'Because you dared to rebel. You're guilty of having defended yourself, of not having been resigned to your punishment. You are guilty of pride and individualism!' This is just a taste of the way obedience is viewed in the seminaries. I could come up with lots of other examples of the cruel stupidity of this repressive system. But generally speaking what it is designed to castrate in the boys who pass through it is their imagination, their ability to think of the future and of their own futures. From this point of view the seminary is a place which anaesthetises, puts to sleep, paralyses the imagination. Getting it back means going back in time in our memories, returning with irrepressible nostalgia to our pre-institutionalisation lives. Just like prisoners do in jail, to stop themselves going mad. Once our seminarian allowed himself to ask his bishop what sort of priest he would be? On hearing this question the bishop flew into a fit of rage and shot back: 'Who cares what sort of priest you'll be! You'll be a priest for all seasons. You should concentrate on adjusting to the needs and demands of the Church.' Another priest and long-term manager of a seminary in the south of Italy, Father Gregorio, carefully explained to me the meaning and nature of the seminary disciplinary system.

> There you are judged on the basis of insignificant details: how you make up your bed, how you shave, if you keep your room tidy. Things like these are used as clues to your fitness to the life of a functionary, signs of use in understanding whether you are an obedient sheep or a troublemaker. 'If you're loyal in the little things you'll be loyal in the big things', I was repeatedly told when I was a theology student. This invalidates everything said about educating the conscience, training for freedom. It's all simply a convenient screen for the totalitarian reality. The real system is one which never misses a chance to punish those who think for themselves, to strike out at those who dissent and 'keep them at the bottom of the pile'. In this context, it is obviously the conformists who do best, the arse lickers, those who keep mum and never criticise their superiors, the deferential, those who never speak up. It doesn't need saying that these are also the falsest and often the sneakiest boys, those most actively involved in a very commonplace activity in the seminaries: snooping. Follow my reasoning: seminaries are disciplinary institutions which hold the keys to the future of each individual boy coming into

them and they use this power to blackmail constantly. Boys are essentially being asked: 'Have you got dreams? Want to make them come true? Are you really keen to be a priest? Know that the keys to your future are in our hands, and if you want to be a priest you have to do as we say.' On this basis it is clear that there's always something to gain from snooping. Snooping helps you get on, it provides guarantees to your superiors that you'll always be on the right side, on the establishment's side, that you'll never make problems. Quite the contrary, you'll help to solve them. This is how a system of generalised mistrust is generated, one in which no-one can fully trust anyone else. The subject of this snooping is everything people say and read, your political orientation. If you want to keep out of trouble, you have to lie, lie constantly. The system invites you to become a colossal habitual liar, a professional liar. And to give in, always give in. To submit, bow your head. When they punish you your superiors are reasoning that you'll give in sooner or later and become a lamb. In fact, as they see it, this disciplinary work protects them from complaints which may come in later, I mean, in the event that a seminarian later fails as priest they will be able to say: 'We tried everything. We punished him many times. We left no stone unturned to make a good priest of him!'

In this context it is thus unsurprising that study and intellectual thinking are not accorded much importance and effectively viewed as risky and suspicious, to be discouraged at all times. 'I'm told that things were better once but it's impossible to study at seminaries now', another young northern Italian priest told me.

In the morning we went to school and in the afternoon they kept us busy with all sorts of activities designed to prevent us from studying: choir rehearsals, coach trips to some saints' day festivities, visits to the sacristy. Anything at all. If I wanted to study I had to find a hiding place. And if they found me they immediately got me doing some practical task such as moving some heavy pot. Sometimes they told us explicitly that 'too much study spoils your faith'. It should also be said that, after the Council, modern theology has taken significant steps away from notions of patriarchy and traditional authority and has thus become the number one enemy of many seminary managers. Ultimately the goal of these latter was to dull our minds, avoid us thinking about the system's defects and the fact that they were fooling us. They wanted to stop us thinking, try to show us that the path we were taking was fatal, a dead end. And told us of a Manichean reality in which very few things are worthwhile (such as communal life with other priests, although we soon found out that the only thing we share is our ruler) and the sugar-coated and camouflaged narrative of a non-existent parish life in which all the rest is terrible, with youth going to pot, atheism spreading like wildfire, and so on. As if God had drawn the curtains on this world and moved elsewhere.

'There is an anti-enlightenment culture in the seminary', priest and seminary teacher Father Maurizio confirms.

The importance of study has dropped considerably in recent years. Seminarians spend around forty-five minutes per day at their books. The rest of the time they 'float in honey' and, as a priest friend of mine says, 'they're taken out to see fictitious things'. In the afternoons they are always out, wasting two days going to Rome to celebrate their bishop being made cardinal, going to a Virgin Mary feast day somewhere or other, listening to wordy speeches by rectors and spiritual fathers, not to speak of night-time worship, etc. I've seen students sit exams with open books in front of them and teachers helping them read its contents. I've heard phone calls from bishops asking stricter teachers not to fail some bone-headed and lazy seminarian or other who the diocese needs and then adding that there's nothing to be gained from being so strict... and so on. The point is that the most frustrated and out-of-touch with real life are the bishops and seminary managers themselves. These are the most cynical of all, the ones telling boys fairy stories and taking them to Disneyland to trick them into remaining idealistic innocents as long as possible. I hate to say it but many trainers are not culturally up to the task, starting with the rectors who dictate the approach and almost always play the part of the bad cop in the game, the one who gets you out in a cold sweat when you're called into his office, the one who gives you the bad news, including the news you fear the most obviously, the decision to expel you from the seminary. The task of the spiritual father, on the other hand, is internal matters. He's the good cop, the one who consoles you, who feeds you some useless mystical solution to your very real problems. Their importance is next to nothing and they're obsolete, past their sell-by date, incapable of providing real spiritual comfort mainly because they have no institutional autonomy and are totally at its beck and call. Ultimately what the spiritual father teaches you most is to hold on, put up with it all, swallow everything that happens to you there and accept it. The strategy they give you is more or less the same: pray a lot, make a few sacrifices and so on. If a rector wants to punish you, your spiritual father can try to soften the punishment. To defend you he'll say something like: he isn't a rebel, he's a good boy, let's give him another chance, send him to the parish for a while and so on. Then there are the bit players: the teachers who are brought in once a year to report on whether or not a boy is studying, whether he's working; parish priests in the boy's parish, whose influence over him is destined to diminish over time; and the vice-rector, an ambiguous figure who seminarians think of as friends because they are young too, because they know how to get on with the boys, because they've worked in youth centres and act like scout leaders. In actual fact, vice-rectors are essentially prison guards, responsible for overseeing the seminarians. On paper they are supposed to be motivators but generally have no specific training and often do serious harm.

Obviously when the time comes, when new young priests come up against the real world 'out there' it can be a terrible shock: some give up, some have breakdowns, some go off the rails, some do worse. Naturally some make it through, discover the value of poverty, really devote themselves to doing good works. Do you know what the ordination mass is called? The one that makes you a priest? It's called 'Saint Liberata', because, from this moment on, you're free. I mean 'free for all'. And this is exactly what happens. You go from total control to total indifference. After ordination priests realise that no-one cared really about them in the upper echelons of the seminary, that there was never any real affection for them from their superiors, that it wasn't true that the control was about making sure they didn't get lost.

This latter point, the feeling of desertion that young priests are left with, is a key one. We'll get back to it in the conclusion to this book. Now we need to get a closer look at our seminarians, get a feel for who they are, what they're looking for and where they come from. This will be the subject of the next chapter.

7 Personal Identity and Clerical Vocation
Who Goes Into a Seminary Today?

To all intents and purposes seminaries are the places in which 'clericality' is fully formed, in which individuals internalise what it means to be part of this very special caste of the elect, the Catholic clergy. Ordination marks the culmination of this journey as the presumed birth of a new, transfigured and sacralised man whose essence is no longer simply human, it is semi-divine.

Let us begin by asking ourselves who these boys going into seminaries are. What are their family and social backgrounds? What is the psychology of these Catholic Church 'elects'?

In the absence of official data my assessment based on ten years or so of enquiry is that many seminarians come from the lower social classes, that – over time – the average age has gone up and, as has been universally noted, that numbers of 'traditionalists' and conservatives, of young people in love with worship, of liturgical matters and flowing robes, with 'lace and frills' – to use an expression coined by a former vice rector – are on the increase. There are more of these young traditionalists than there were even just a short time ago. The years of anti-establishment struggle and the Vatican II led to a modernised clergy, including externally, and the disappearance of cassocks, crucifixes, rings and collars. Many priests began dressing normally, keeping the appurtenances of the priestly class to a minimum. During the papacy of John Paul II this trend would seem to have been inverted and tradition returned to fashion in the clergy. As regards the French clergy, Josselin Tricou has spoken of a 'John Paul II generation' which joined the clergy during Wojtyla's papacy from 1978 to 2005, in the wake of the 'great crisis' which saw a great exodus from the priesthood in the 1960s and 70s. 'Generally considered to be a pivotal generation from the point of view of "the reconstitution of the priestly ideal" (Béraud 2006),' wrote Tricou (2018, p. 6), 'these priests mostly embody what Philippe Portier (2012) calls an "identity-based Catholicism" in reaction to the "open Catholicism" that was brought to the fore in the 1970s and 1980s'. As we will see, the clerical garb question is bound up with the sexual identity of many of these priests.

Seminarians' family backgrounds also seem to display certain common features. This is a theme which has attracted the attention of a great many of the psychologists who have studied the clerical mentality. As early as the

DOI: 10.4324/9781003426271-7

1980s the authors of research into the clergy commissioned by the North American National Conference of Catholic Bishops (Hoge, Potvin and Ferry 1984, p. 23) spoke of the presence of dominant mother figures, both actual and subconscious (i.e. the mother as a female ideal), as one of the most significant features of seminarians' lives and personalities. Kochansky and Cohen (2007, 45–46), on the other hand, have noted that it is mothers of priests who tend to idealise their priest sons while these latter were

> frequently deflated and/or rendered unstable by their fathers, through excessive, sometimes sadistic criticism [...] often including the child's being insufficiently masculine or even effeminate. The mothers of these boys, in turn, often felt and conveyed disappointment in their husbands, whom they portrayed as emotionally distant and insensitive and/or weak, and they often sought and established a special, sometimes relatively overtly eroticized closeness with their sons.

These same authors (Kochansky and Cohen 2007, p. 47) also note that 'certain demands of the institutional Church, such as the promise of celibacy, reinforce the preexisting and longstanding oedipal bond with their mothers that characterizes a certain subgroup of priests'. In some cases 'for some immature priests, biological mother, Holy Mother Church, and Mary the Mother of God, merged into one sacred, untouchable yet demanding maternal configuration' (Frawley-O'Dea 2007, p. 67, see also Cozzens 2000, pp. 76–77).

Adoration of the mother-son bond is seriously justified, by priests, in the following terms: 'the Church's historical relationship with women has been increasingly to theologize and legislate mouthy, unruly Eve out, replacing her with an increasingly submissive Mary the Virgin Mother' (Walker 2007, p. 224). Idealisation of the figure of the Virgin Mary, together with that of their own mothers – modelled on an entirely masculine vision – was ultimately a powerful form of misogyny (Frawley-O'Dea 2007) leading to a comparative devaluation of all other women, of the female sex as a whole (Sipe 2003, p. 84). The chauvinist structure of the Church, essentially itself a possessive and totalising mother, reinforces such feelings and justifies priests' right to exercise power over all other women (Sipe 2003, p. 173). Incidentally, it should be noted that misogyny is a key feature of the Catholic Church's organisational culture and fundamental to its identity. As the greatest international expert in clerical sexuality, Richard Sipe, has observed (2003, p. 85, see also Schlüsser-Florenza 1983) in Catholic culture all dominant figures, all people of power, starting with God the Father and Jesus the Son all the way to father and bishop are men and 'an enduring model for priests is the Roman paterfamilias (or feudal lord) who held power over the life and death of his household' (Sipe 2003, p. 85). This aversion to women, seen as sources of untold danger to priests, is explicitly stressed during priests' theological training, frequently by way of readings of the most misogynist excerpts from the Christian patristics (Jordan 2000, p. 161). Ultimately, the moral behind much of Christian discourse on gender is that

> men are wounded and suffer because they fall prey to women's sexual power with the ultimate result the death of the God/man. Virginity and submission to the male are idealized as feminine expiation, just as male celibacy is constituted as a sign of superior power and godlikeness
>
> (Walker 2007, p. 225).

My interviews revealed a similar frequently 'special' relationship between aspirant priests and their mothers.

For example, the trainers and psychologists I interviewed were virtually unanimous in portraying seminarians as having extremely present mothers, some of whom are morbidly attached to their sons and eager for them to join the seminaries.

'Seminarians' mothers are all alike', said Father Fabio, vice rector of a large Northern Italian seminary for over a decade,

> they are in love with their sons and delighted that they will, if everything goes according to plan and they do not give up the cassock, have no other women in their lives. They are effectively happy that, if they cannot themselves get into bed with their adored sons at least no one else will.

'Their attachment to their mothers is truly scary', confided Father Matteo, another educator,

> to the extent that we sometimes have to take action, cut those apron strings, keep them away from their mothers for a little, at least physically. For example, we have sometimes advised the bishop to send young priests somewhere a long away from home right after ordination, where their mothers cannot follow them.

Proud mothers in love with their priest sons are also frequently one of the main obstacles to them leaving the clergy, abandoning a frequently unhappy life replete with hypocrisy and lies. Many priests or former priests have confessed that the greatest terror for them is, or was, 'breaking their mothers' hearts', inflicting a huge and undeserved blow on the women who have done so much for them, an even greater worry than unemployment or the loss of the status bound up with the priesthood.

It is often only after the deaths of their mothers that priests feel able to cast off their disguises and be open about their sexualities. In confirmation of this Richard Sipe (2003, p. 157) reported the case of a 40-something homosexual priest, a patient of his, who remained impeccably celibate, after a few youthful indiscretions before joining the seminary, until his mother's death. After this he instantly got into a relationship, which he himself described as compulsive, with a notoriously gay parishioner. Once his grief passed, so did this sexual compulsion and he gradually returned to his earlier chastity.

In actual fact, this perennially dominant mother figure is not always a loving protector. Sometimes the exact opposite is the case, and their mothers are seen by priests as rejecting and emotionally inadequate (Sipe 2003, p. 273). Sipe argued that, in such cases, priests' emotional demands are channelled into the Church, as Holy Mother, to compensate for the shortcomings of a motherly love not up to the expectations and needs of suffering sons. What I myself have encountered in such cases is a profoundly ambivalent love-hate mother-son relationship of powerful dependence and desire for autonomy.

All these elements are there in the symbiotic and infantile relationship with his mother described by Father Luigi, a 40-something southern Italian priest who lives with his parents and is incapable of deciding even when to return home at night on his own. Even when he has an appointment with his therapist or is seeing a friend Father Luigi has to make up a story about a non-existent meeting to avoid his mother 'telling him off'.

> I do what she says because I'm incapable of doing otherwise, but at the same time I detest her because the way she treats me saddens and depresses me. I've noticed that she even goes as far as rummaging around in the mass donations box. I'd love to break free of her but I just can't. If I were really to put a distance between us, if I put my fantasies into practice and freed myself of her, I'd immediately feel guilty.

The case of Father Franco, a central Italian priest, is equally revealing in this regard. He told of coming from an ultra-Catholic family with an older brother who is also a priest and a younger one who has also been a seminarian for some time. Father Franco's parents are highly religious people who were part of a large ecclesiastical movement for some time. In the family it is their mother who rules the roost, a woman who Franco described as 'overbearing and possessive, always complaining about her husband and whose attitude to "masculinity", namely my father, is difficult.' 'My mother', he continued,

> definitely pushed me and my two brothers into the seminary. With the support of a priest who was then rector of the seminary in our town, a highly charismatic figure who spent a great deal of time at our house, my mother continually pushed us in the direction of the priesthood. Like my brothers before and after me I went into a minor seminary, without any special inclination for it and attracted if anything by its leisure opportunities, by the chance to do plenty of sport and live with my peers, but to an even greater extent to live up to my mother's expectations and escape her constant attempts to manipulate me, to poke her nose into my life, her bad moods, sulks, the pain revolving around her

marital life and our family. In the years which followed I often got a very strong urge to leave, to get away, to give it up. But as soon as I cautiously touched on the subject with my mother and her friend the rector they reacted so harshly that I couldn't go on with it. They practically wouldn't speak to me, they 'turned off the light' and ignored me altogether. This was just too painful for me and I retracted the whole thing, told them I'd changed my mind and didn't want to leave the path to priesthood. My mother forgave me and was nice to me again, showing me lots of affection. Even after I became a priest, at least in the first few years, she watched over me to ensure I wasn't seeing women. To get away from her at least to some extent I had to get thousands of miles away from her, in Africa, where she couldn't get to me.

This ambivalent relationship between priests and their mothers is even more striking and painful in the case of Marcello, a 50-something former priest from the north of Italy.

Mine was a deeply religious family. The decisive event, which marked me for life, was the tragic and sudden death from illness of my father, when I was only seven. He was a jolly man, full of life, a playful person. He loved messing around with us children, giving us plenty of love and play. His death brought my childhood to a sudden end. My mother, a difficult and moody woman, fell into a deep depression and obsessively religious manias began preying on her mind. She began spending all her time with priests and religious groups. My decision to go into the priesthood, to join a minor seminary at the age of 13 was, in many ways, the result of an uncontrollable desire to get away, to escape that painful and oppressive situation. I thought that if I went into a seminary I'd finally be living my own life and getting away from my mother and her madness. I thought I'd finally be able to breathe freely, without her breathing down my neck.

During my interview with Marcello, however, it emerged that going into a seminary was also a way of averting any chance of marriage and thus the possibility of bereavement and the suffering experienced by his mother. It was also to fulfil his mother's expectations, realise her dream of a son in the priesthood. 'My mother', continued this former priest, 'is a frosty, unaffectionate, always aloof woman. It was only by going into the priesthood that I got some affection from her.' While he was in his seminary Marcello's mother followed him everywhere.

She wormed her way into the convent next door to the seminary to keep an eye on me. When I was ordained and sent to be a vice parish priest she'd turn up everywhere, even at a little party I held in my flat once. She checked that I wasn't seeing women, oversaw my chastity, drove away any women she thought were hanging around me, sometimes rudely.

When Marcello told her that he was leaving the priesthood, she responded very negatively indeed, telling her son that she never wanted to see him again, refusing to meet his wife and daughter and taking him out of her will altogether. Marcello saw her again only many years later when, as an elderly woman, she got Alzheimer's disease and the rest of the family asked for his help.

> On alternate weeks, until we put her into a home, my mother came to stay at my house. We couldn't let her sleep alone because she might have hurt herself, so I decided to sleep in the same room as her. It was on one of these occasions that it happened, that she tried to have sex with me. She touched herself, asked me to kiss her and to make love to her. I know that it was the disease speaking but for me it was a revelation which my analyst later confirmed in full. Thinking about what happened on those nights I realised that I had always been an object of desire for my mother and going into the priesthood I had gone along with her possession fantasies, her chilling exclusivity demands.

If their mothers are, in some way, key, dominant figures for many seminarians, their fathers are often weak and absent or negative, strict and despotic figures. This has been widely confirmed by the international scientific literature (Dinter 2003), with Hoge (2005) arguing that many priests' fathers are alcoholics. Celenza (2005), a psychoanalyst, discovered, on the basis of therapeutic work with the clergy, that many priests lost their fathers young through death or abandonment or they were emotionally aloof or even humiliated by their wives, i.e. the priests' mothers. The latter group sometimes idealised priests, frequently their parish priests, at the expense of their husbands (Frawley-O'Dea 2007). 'Becoming a priest', Frawley-O'Dea suggests (2007, p. 102), 'at one level, can be seen therefore as an unconscious attempt to become the man the mother really loved while finding a new father in the Church – God, bishops, pastors.'

For many young men joining the seminary their parish or other priests are a positive paternal ideal – understanding and encouraging – and often become a model to follow, to emulate. And the same is true later of their seminary superiors, spiritual directors, bishops or other (especially eminent) older priests (Kochansky and Cohen 2009). Clearly it does not need to be underlined that, just as we saw in Carlo's story, there are a multitude of risks inherent in these paternalistic relationships (Kochansky and Cohen 2009).

The overall psychological profile of seminarians outlined by the psychologists I have spoken to is one of profoundly immature, highly fragile individuals frightened by the idea of living in a competitive, meritocratic world. 'Aspiring priests', noted Dr Rossi, a well-known central Italian psychologist who has worked as seminary consultant for many years,

> are often boys who believe, more or less consciously, that they do not have what it takes for decent personal and social lives. For them the

cassock is a way out of this dilemma. They believe that it will give them the identity and social role that they would not otherwise be capable of obtaining. In the last analysis, I have to admit, they are 'losers'; people otherwise destined for social failure. The Church dredge up what is left after the best have been taken.

In the opinion of a further psychologist, a priest with many decades of therapeutic experience and an in-depth knowledge of the Italian Catholic world, what clerical recruitment methods prioritise is not the genuineness of candidates' faith (which is never truly assessed) but rather their willingness to obey and conform to doctrine. 'They get in if they show that they are obedient and efficient underlings', this elderly priest-psychologist told me, if they are

> easy to transform into institutional agents, conformist bureaucrats willing to deny the evident if organisational loyalty requires it. None of the rest counts for anything for those selecting aspirant priests. And, in fact, everyone knows that there is a busy 'seminar market' packed with opportunities. If a boy is expelled from a seminary, perhaps because his personality profile is disturbed or he falls short in the sexual sphere, he may very well be taken in by another one. And do you know what such decisions depend on? On whether or not a bishop needs priests and is thus willing to let the guard down and take a few rejects, the worst elements, to keep the show on the road. For many bishops the only criteria which really counts seems to be numbers, volumes. 'The more the better' seems to be their slogan. But there are even worst cases: the bishops who seek out the rotten apples, the rejects, in the hope of turning them into totally subservient minions who owe everything to him, as they would never otherwise be able to be priests and anything can be asked of them.

The experiences of another psychologist, also at length consultant at many seminaries, corroborate this with a similar view. 'Priests are generally tragically insecure', says Dr Bianchi,

> people who were always on the margins in groups before joining seminaries, occupying a peripheral and marginal role in conversations and interactions with others. People like this think they can count for something only as priests. It needs to be said: the Church is a phenomenal social elevator for mediocre people, one of very few institutions in which boys who aren't worth much can achieve positions of power. And it is precisely this power over consciences which gives priests that thrill which often turns into perversion, into delusions of grandeur. Feelings of control over other people's lives, taking confession, being people's spiritual guide often leads to them losing their heads, jeopardising their personality balance. They end up disparaging others, belittling and scorning

them in order finally to feel better about themselves. Clearly this is the only strategy possible for people with very low self-esteem.

And I would add that it is clear that this is the very same strategy bishops employ with unruly priest-sheep. These are features which did not escape Drewermann's sophisticated theological psychoanalysis (1995) which argued that young seminarians are imbued with a great sense of hopelessness without knowing what is behind it. This feeling evaporates when they finally discover that, in becoming priests, they can stake their claim to a higher vocation, be part of 'the elect'.

The overall picture drawn by psychologists seems to me entirely plausible: seminarians are often lost boys desperately seeking existential sanctuary. If this were not the case, how – in this day and age – could people be persuaded to agree to live in places from which women are banned; where you need to ask permission to do anything, even the most innocent; where your mobile phone can be taken away from you; where, until a few years ago, being found with a pornographic magazine meant being turned out onto the street for a night or suspension of weekend home leave for protracted periods?

The immediate effect of being treated like children in adulthood, well after the age of twenty, is to strengthen feelings of dependence and destroy self-esteem and all feelings of personal autonomy and effectiveness. 'One of the most telling ways in which one's economy of action can be disrupted', wrote Goffman in *Asylums*

> is the obligation to request permission or supplies for minor activities that one can execute on one's own on the outside, such as smoking, shaving, going to the toilet, telephoning, spending money or mailing letters. This obligation not only puts the individual in a submissive or suppliant role 'unnatural' for an adult but also opens up his line of action to interceptions by staff.
> (Goffman 1961, p. 41)

Those submitting voluntarily to regimes such as this, choosing to enter total institutions, feel 'a willful desire to be stripped and cleansed of personal will' (Goffman 1961, p. 47).

Dr Bianchi's words, and the views of Goffman, conjure up general rules relating to the irresistible appeal strong institutions have for the weak. It is a universal mechanism which applies to all authoritarian and highly hierarchical institutions. Seminaries are the Catholic location in which this authoritarian culture is passed on: inside them boys are protected and coddled by an institution which takes on board all their needs, providing for all their requirements, in exchange, naturally, for their total and unconditional obedience and absolute loyalty.

In a nutshell, the typical psycho-social profile of a seminarian outlined by the experts I interviewed is ultimately a boy from a non-affluent family, frequently with an extremely overbearing, possessive, castrating and sex-phobic mother and a weak and absent or authoritarian and violent father, and an immature personality with serious inter-personal problems, extremely low self-esteem and, very often, a marked difficulty accepting his own sexual orientation. For some psychologists I have met, these last two characteristics – weak self-esteem and uncertainty regarding one's sexual preferences – significantly correlate. 'Many people with low self-esteem', Dr Verdi explained,

> fear, frequently wrongly, that they are gay. They say to themselves that, as they are desperate cases they must also be homosexual. It is a full-blown phobia. These boys need help, support and care. But the Church responds by making loyal soldiers of them, on the basis of their fragility. And, effectively, those selecting, training and managing them in the seminaries are, in turn, yesterday's misfits and failures.

Once in the seminaries and during training, for the reasons we will look at later on, the young recruits learn that singular moral code which labels drop outs and losers those ruled by their emotions; the ingenuous, those who obey the letter of the law, or take it rather too seriously, trust the next man too much or fail to cultivate cynicism and diffidence; and the overly honest or the imprudent, the ones who get caught. The winners are the cunning ones, who learn quickly how to 'work the system' (Goffman, 1961), the hypocrites and professional liars.

I'll bring this chapter to an end with the highly revealing and bitter words of a memoir text written specially for me by a middle-aged northern Italian priest.

> I lived in a seminary for thirteen years in the 1980s and 90s. It was a period which saw numbers of seminarians increase in the space of just a few years to over 400. No-one, not even me, thought at the time that the society we belonged to was disoriented, confused and often careless, leaving no room for complex teenage egos which were rejected as useless and superfluous fantasies. A place such as this can only produce candidates for pastoral care incapable of looking real life in the face because they themselves are outsiders to the real world they are to take on. What I remember most about the seminary is having passed years of my life with dozens of priests and hundreds of seminarians thinking about, and attending spiritual retreats on, priestly fraternity and community spirit, celibacy, poverty and obedience. What I am sure about is that I wasted a great deal of time, that all I did was listen to doublespeak, hear broken promises and see the whole hypocritical house of cards expertly cloaked by ritual-liturgical self-righteousness.

8 Obsession and Guilt
Seminarians' Troubled Sex Lives

The central importance of sex and love in the warp and weave of seminary organisation is tangible first and foremost in the fact that talking about such matters is entirely taboo in future priests' cloistered lives. Unlike every other present-day venue of social interaction, sex and love are never talked about in seminaries with the sole possible exception of the context in which the moral precepts of Catholic doctrine are discussed, and then in strictly theoretical terms. The institutions which train the clergy take it entirely for granted that aspiring priests are fully aware of the need to live fully sex-less lives, not to fall in love except with their own high office and that their entire lives should be devoted to serving the institution and their flocks. It is officially and publicly assumed by the Church that celibacy and chastity, whilst certainly challenging, are entirely possible at least for the select few of 'superior men' capable, on the strength of their special 'divine virtue', of achieving a state of stable abstinence from carnal contact and love with a reasonable degree of serenity. Those of the new recruits who feel – or turn out to be – unable to live up to such expectations and dictates are expected to leave the seminaries as soon as possible of their own free will and take some other existential path, in accordance with God's will. This is the official line.[1]

But the reality is very different. What there can be no doubt of is that the sexual and emotional sphere is the key stage on which seminarians' allegiance to the institution is played out. On what other grounds might seminarians be ousted from the seminaries? Because they don't study hard enough? Because they miss a few exams? Because they miss one too many masses? Because they realise they don't love the Lord enough? And on what grounds do priests leave the priesthood at any age? Perhaps on the basis of some terrible crisis of faith?

The answer to all these questions is always and in all circumstances 'no'. All the potential causes cited – study, mass, prayer, attitude to God – are decidedly of secondary importance in priests' training.

In the vast majority, if not all, cases the reasons priests leave, or are expelled from, the seminaries and the priesthood are a matter of their failure to abide by the mandatory celibacy and chastity rules. Naturally this does

DOI: 10.4324/9781003426271-8

not mean that any violation of these rules leads to voluntary or non-voluntary abandonment of the seminary or the priesthood. Many violations are, in fact, tolerated by the institution or ignored by aspiring priests themselves. But it is, in any event, almost invariably for problems bound up with this sphere of life that the break with seminary or priestly life takes place. In a great many cases, in fact, the task of trainers is to find a wise and unobtrusive solution to complications bound up with sexuality and love. It is above all in this field that their managerial skills are to be judged, together with their ability to manage organisational emergencies. As Protestant theologian Erich Fuchs has argued 'it is the rigorous management of sexuality that qualifies the authority of the cleric as well as the obedience of the laity' (cited in Tricou 2018, p. 2).

Let us now examine how the acquisition of mandatory celibacy translates concretely into everyday life in the seminaries.

I have already touched on the first – informal but ultra-strict – institutional rule, the linguistic taboo. Sex and love (obviously in the sense of romantic, not universal, love or love of God, for one's mother or siblings) in official seminary life simply do not exist. No mention is made of them whatsoever. Such matters must never be touched on, at least in public and in reference to seminarians' private lives. They crop up only, to a greater or lesser extent, in private conversations between classmates or tête-à-tête between seminarians and their spiritual fathers, in private or in confession. Otherwise, in more general terms, in seminarians' theological training there is simply no place for real life experiences or the emotional plane. The educational process and the language used in it is entirely abstract and centred on the rules, on how things should be, the moral laws to be abided by and by which others are to be required to abide (this has also been corroborated by the large number of Irish priests taking part in Keenan's important study [2012, p. 140]). As Father Nunzio, a central Italian priest, explained:

> In the many years I spent in the seminary, both minor and major, I was never given any sexual education. So during my adolescence I never received any support or information of use in helping me manage my sexuality in my everyday life. Sex-related matters were avoided at the seminary like all other questions related to young men's psycho-social development, such as independence, getting on with one's peers, the desire for intellectual growth and so on. In such a climate our imaginations ran riot, life's normal glitches were blown up out of all proportion and our emotional difficulties in our relations with our classmates risked becoming obsessive. Preparation for celibacy almost always took the exclusive form of entirely theoretical sex-phobic precepts. During the weekly meditations guided by our spiritual father (often at seven in the morning) it was reiterated that the Church bans all sexual relations outside marriage and not for the purpose of procreation and exalts chastity as a way of getting closer to God. Rejection of sex was justified on religious

and moral grounds, i.e. that it produces immature individuals and blocks the development of psycho-social equilibrium. We were told that we had to sublimate everything and find other avenues for our energies. In the major seminary such considerations turned into full-blown teachings involving reading excerpts from the canon law code on the subject of chastity and celibacy.

The eradication of sex from the public debate also marshalled the ascetic saints as models to be emulated. Father Armando, for example, confided the following:

> In my seminary the confessors and spiritual fathers we were required to meet every two weeks urged us to follow the example of St Aloysius de Gonzaga, who is frequently depicted with a lily symbolising purity, innocence and candour. If I think, today, of St Aloysius de Gonzaga and others like him who mortified their own flesh to 'tame their carnal urges' I can't help thinking that there was something sick in it. Perhaps these saints were naturally psychopathic or perhaps they became so as a result of the abstinence and continual torture they inflicted on themselves to drive out desire. Because abstinence combined with masochistic practices – no-one can deny this today – can lead to physical and cerebral damage which can trigger madness and schizophrenia, syndromes which the biographers of such saints viewed as 'ecstasy' or 'mystical crises' and sometimes hailed as miracles.

In any event, repressing what is never named, what is kept out of the public sphere is, in the minor seminaries, cruel, ineffective but above all ambiguous, constantly fluctuating between punishment and desire, prohibition and seduction. As Father Ilario's account makes clear on the subject of the way his spiritual father watched over the chastity of the young seminarians in their high school years:

> He sometimes came to visit us in the evenings, coming in quite suddenly in the dark and pulled away our sheets with a rapid gesture to see what was going on underneath. He sometimes sat down on the bed with one of us, in the darkness of the dormitory lit only by a weak night light. When his visit was over he urged us all, in a whisper, to sleep with our arms over our blankets. A few years later one of my classmates of the day went public about the terrible abuse he had suffered at the hands of that spiritual father. It is only now that I can see, finally, why that man laid us bare so determinedly, what it was he was hoping to see.

This radical linguistic censure, the ban on talking about sex and seminarians' emotional lives, obviously did not really make such matters go away. In a nutshell, not talking about something does not mean it is not there. Quite the opposite, the outcome of the non-presence of sex and the emotions in the public seminary sphere is that it features even larger in the private sphere, in the institution's underground, clandestine life (Goffman 1961). In other words, attempting to deny the very existence of sex makes it central to everything. 'The obsession with sexual surveillance', notes Jordan (2000, p. 168) 'deforms aspects of seminary life that don't seem to have anything particularly to do with sex – for instance the sense of personal privacy and the possibility of relaxed friendship.' Total silence on the subject of sex in the public seminary sphere is broken only in confession and conversations with seminarians' spiritual fathers where sex plays a centre stage, often explicit and obsessive, role. It is a world based on guilt and later expiation, as the account of an Irish priest told by Keenan expresses very effectively (2012, p. 135):

> [In the seminary] sex was dirty and sinful and we needed to purify ourselves. The over-abiding experience I had as regards sexuality was that it was sinful [...]. It was the forbidden fruit...it was a struggle for survival about the guilt factor. Every week we had two lectures from a priest from the Diocese, who is long since dead, and I tell you everything about sex was bad, bad, bad. Then you also had the hygiene and sanitation lectures, which spoke of going out with women you could get VD [venereal disease]. I often went to confession three or four times a week just to feel ok...would I or wouldn't I, did I or didn't I? What did I think? Never about touching, always about thinking...I didn't know how to get rid of this thing. I was ashamed of myself for having to go and repeat the same things in confession over and over and over again. It was all about sexuality. I believe we lived in the seminary as though there was no other commandment...there was only one thing in morality and that was sex...nothing else mattered. There was nothing else moral. Everything else was just something else. So the word morality was sex. Nothing to do with justice, nothing to do with any other thing. It had to do with sex.

'Underlife' is the inevitable consequence of repression. Goffman (2001) noted, in fact, that total institutions always succeed in controlling the lives of those living in them. These latter cannot, without the complete annihilation of their personalities and the total loss of their freedom and individuality, avoid setting in motion a frequently covert and indirect form of resistance to institutional demands.

Goffman (1961, pp. 54–55) called these 'secondary adjustments', referring to

> practices that do not directly challenge staff but allow inmates to obtain forbidden satisfactions or to obtain permitted ones by forbidden means [...] Secondary adjustments provide the inmate with important evidence

that he is still his own man, with some control of his environment; sometimes a secondary adjustment becomes also a kind of lodgement for the self, a churinga in which the soul is felt to reside.

I believe that, in total institutions entered voluntarily, such as seminaries, secondary adjustments take on complex and ambiguous forms of simultaneous defeat and resistance. More specifically, on one hand secondary adjustments supply seminarians with the grounds for everyday self-inflicted moral crucifixion as they themselves see them as serious violations of the law, full-blown crimes against God accompanied by a huge sense of guilt and, on the other – and seminarians only grasp this years later – they are the only way open to them to keep alive some form of personal autonomy, the most concrete marks of an authentic existence not completely subsumed by their role. Thus, whilst they are experienced subjectively by aspiring priests as agonising and shameful, as a painful necessity imposed on them by nature, these secondary adjustments effectively serve to keep them alive as free, thinking people, as autonomous and vital human beings.

Clearly such adaptations relate primarily to sex and the behavioural sphere bound up with sexuality formally banned by the institution. The example of solitary sex will make my meaning clearer.

The most commonplace sexual activity in seminaries, and thus the primary object of control, is naturally the onanistic, solitary practice of masturbation. Point 2.352 of the Catechism of the Catholic Church reads:

> By *masturbation* is to be understood the deliberate stimulation of the genital organs in order to derive sexual pleasure. [...] Both the Magisterium of the Church, in the course of a constant tradition, and the moral sense of the faithful have been in no doubt and have firmly maintained that masturbation is an intrinsically and gravely disordered action. [...] The deliberate use of the sexual faculty, for whatever reason, outside of marriage is essentially contrary to its purpose.
> (Catechism of the Catholic Church 2016)

For here sexual pleasure is sought outside of 'the sexual relationship which is demanded by the moral order and in which the total meaning of mutual self-giving and human procreation in the context of true love is achieved.' The text concludes with a few hints on circumstances mitigating its seriousness. It continues: 'To form an equitable judgment about the subjects' moral responsibility and to guide pastoral action, one must take into account the affective immaturity, force of acquired habit, conditions of anxiety or other psychological or social factors that lessen, if not even reduce to a minimum, moral culpability.'

For Catholic doctrine, then, masturbation is always, although to varying degrees, a sinful, immoral act. And this is even more true for seminarians and priests. It would, however, seem, that this rule is frequently disobeyed, if we are to believe Richard Sipe, who wrote that 80 percent of priests masturbate regularly. Sipe himself refers to a 1969 survey by Dr William Masters which testifies to close to 100% of priests masturbating (in his sample exactly 198 out of 200 and Dr Masters argued that the remaining two did not understand the question (Sipe 2003, p. 57). A further figure is the 50 homosexual priests interviewed by sexologist Richard Wagner (1981), 47 of whom admitted masturbating with an average frequency of a grand total of three times higher than that reported by Kinsey[2] in his famous report on American sexuality (Jordan 2000, p. 104). In his important work *Functionaries of God*, Eugen Drewermann (1995) argued that

> in the midst of a plethora of obligatorily grey and joyless duties masturbation comes across paradoxically as the sole place of rest. Many clerics – the few with the courage to speak up – recount having always had to masturbate to cope with powerful work-related problems, to get over their anxiety.

It was once again Sipe (2003) who noted – citing Freud and others – that masturbation can take on both physiological and pathological traits. The pathological trait cited by Sipe is the sexual excitement, even masturbation, reported by many priests whilst listening to confession. The circumstance (confirmed by the majority of my own interviewees) that for many seminarians masturbation is anything but a pleasant practice is equally pathological, with masturbation being described as a painful, physiological necessity or the source of huge moral suffering. This is confirmed by 25 years of confessional experience by one of the older priests interviewed in Ireland by Marie Keenan (2012, 135): 'The two aspects of sexuality, this priest confided, that were particularly troubling (for priests) during their seminary education were again purity and now masturbation.'

Ultimately,

> in traditional moral theology, masturbation is an unnatural act and hence more serious than heterosexual intercourse. But in seminary life masturbation was much more frequent than heterosexual intercourse – and much more excusable. It could happen much more quickly and alone, within the walls, without long planning or the violation of other seminary rules, say, about enclosure. Masturbation could follow on the rush of desire from an erotic dream in the drowsy half-sleep of early morning. It could become confused with that other object of expert concern: the nocturnal emission.
>
> (Jordan 2000, p. 163)

Almost all the priests who agreed to speak to me on the subject reported masturbation experiences at the seminary accompanied by great feelings of guilt and sometimes self-mutilation fantasies, as in the account of a priest patient of Drewermann's who spoke of 'wanting to tear it off for ever every time I did it'.

Father Patrizio talked of feeling terribly 'dirty' after masturbating. 'When I was at the minor seminary', he said,

> we slept in dormitories and the bathrooms were the only place in which we could touch ourselves. And right there, exactly over the toilet bowl, our superiors had a sign saying 'God is watching you' fixed to the wall. When I'd finished, after ejaculation, I felt terrible. I begged God to forgive me, but I couldn't help myself. If I hadn't masturbated I would have gone mad. When I confessed my spiritual father listened calmly to what I had to say and asked me how often I'd done it.

Another priest, Father Armando, remembers having discovered onanism at seminary middle school and having been obsessed at length with the effects of each single act of masturbation. 'It was a terrible torment', he remembers.

> I thought that if I had masturbated I wouldn't be able to take communion and would have first to go to confession. And as I touched myself practically every day I had got myself into a sort of monstrous vicious circle, a habitual toing and froing in which I touched myself and had to confess. The priest who took my confession didn't react but I felt trapped and crushed. I felt torn apart, locked up in a sort of psychic jail. Eventually I myself broke out of this circle: obviously I kept on masturbating but I decided to stop going to confession, not to worry, and to keep going to communion all the same.

Perhaps the most significant testimony I gathered on this very delicate subject was that of Father Aldo who said he had never masturbated for pleasure 'but always out of necessity, because [he] couldn't do otherwise or [his] head would have exploded'.

> And [there was] always a huge sense of guilt. On some special occasions I got into a full-blown challenge with myself. For example, a couple of times, during Lent, I solemnly promised the Virgin Mary that I would not touch myself for the whole forty days up to Easter. Obviously I didn't manage it. I was so disgusted with myself afterwards that I didn't mention it in confession. Neither did I talk to others about it. Because I experienced it as a huge sin. I felt unworthy of Jesus. The Lord had called me to the priesthood and my response was to betray him by touching myself constantly. Yes, I experienced it as a betrayal, as a crime against God, proof of just how disgusting I was.

The seminary authorities, on their part, did everything they could to limit it (with very disappointing results, as we have seen). An example is Father Arturo's memories of when masturbation was talked of we were told that the whole Christian tradition considered it a serious and intrinsic sin and, when committed with full consciousness and consent, a mortal sin. Our superiors saw masturbation as a serious problem which we had to free ourselves of before we took our final vows or were made deacons: the absence of masturbation was considered a requisite for ordination or final vows. The spiritual strategy recommended to us was 'ruling over the senses', that is, when we had obscene thoughts we were to get back as quickly as possible from the world of sexual fantasy to the real world. Halting our imaginations with an act of will. The strategies they advised us to use consisted of undertaking some intense spiritual activity (mass and confession), saying an ejaculatory prayer or a rosary or simply distracting ourselves, doing something else, such as a spiritual reading, visiting a sanctuary, going for a walk, studying or some such thing. We were told that we needed to have left such practices behind for at least a year before our last vows or the deaconry. After our 'fall' (i.e. masturbation) we were told that we had to rise above it right away and seek divine forgiveness with personal repentance. Obviously seminarians had to have spiritual leaders to speak to alone at least once a month and a confessor who they were required to confess to every fortnight. Shifting from one confessor to another was banned.

On the crucial modern terrain of the construction of the self and the – not only sexual – identity-shaping process (Laqueur 2003; Stengers and Van Necl 2001), then, this was seminarians' first experience of failure to build a chaste and institutionally compliant self. The initial response of these young people, especially the most ingenuous, was frequently to take all blame for their lack of success, to see themselves as inadequate, incapable, perhaps even unsuited to keeping their promises of being 'God's men', Catholic functionaries up to the expectations made of them. Over time, as we will see, such feelings were set aside and secondary adjustments such as masturbation take on entirely different meanings.

Notes

1 For a detailed description of the official criteria used in the recruitment and training of priests, see the document published by the Dicastery for the Clergy in 2016 entitled *The Gift of the Priestly Vocation* (Congregation for the Clergy, 2016).
2 The comparison with the Kinsey Report is the work of Wagner (1981). I have simply reported it here.

9 Homophobia and Homophilia in the Seminaries
Two Faces of a Single Coin

In 2005 the Congregation for Catholic Education published what turned out to be a highly controversial *Instruction Concerning the Criteria for the Discernment of Vocations with Regard to Persons with Homosexual Tendencies in View of Their Admission to the Seminary and to Holy Orders.*[1] Its introduction referred to the need for urgent action on the issue. The document later cited the Catechism and its well-known distinction between 'homosexual acts' and 'homosexual tendencies', with the former being grave sins, 'intrinsically immoral and contrary to the natural law'; 'deep-seated homosexual tendencies, which are found in a number of men and women, are also objectively disordered'. 'In the light of such teaching', the document continued,

> this Dicastery, in accord with the Congregation for Divine Worship and the Discipline of the Sacraments, believes it necessary to state clearly that the Church, while profoundly respecting the persons in question, cannot admit to the seminary or to holy orders those who practise homosexuality, present deep-seated homosexual tendencies or support the so-called 'gay culture'. Such persons, in fact, find themselves in a situation that gravely hinders them from relating correctly to men and women. One must in no way overlook the negative consequences that can derive from the ordination of persons with deep-seated homosexual tendencies.

Having set out the regulations, the *Instruction* immediately specifies an exception to it:

> Different, however, would be the case in which one were dealing with homosexual tendencies that were only the expression of a transitory problem – for example, that of an adolescence not yet superseded. Nevertheless, such tendencies must be clearly overcome at least three years before ordination to the diaconate.

Thus, on paper at least, boys who are uncertain of their sexual orientation can be admitted to the seminaries as long as such doubts are resolved at least

DOI: 10.4324/9781003426271-9

three years before they are ordained as deacons and thus effectively after their two years in the seminary.

The next section of the *Instruction* explained how the directive is to be applied, clarifying that it is not simply a matter of aspiring priests' subjective feelings of vocation and that it is the task of the ecclesiastical authorities to decide who can be ordained and who is to be expelled from the seminaries. Aspiring priests must be morally irreproachable, argued the document, and all ecclesiastical authorities (bishops, spiritual directors, confessors) must be called on to contribute to identifying individuals truly suited to becoming 'ministers of Christ'.

> It goes without saying that the candidate himself has the primary responsibility for his own formation. He must offer himself trustingly to the discernment of the Church, of the Bishop who calls him to orders, of the rector of the seminary, of his spiritual director and of the other seminary educators to whom the Bishop or major superior has entrusted the task of forming future priests. It would be gravely dishonest for a candidate to hide his own homosexuality in order to proceed, despite everything, towards ordination. Such a deceitful attitude does not correspond to the spirit of truth, loyalty and openness that must characterize the personality of him who believes he is called to serve Christ and his Church in the ministerial priesthood.

This clear closing of the seminary doors to homosexuals has also more recently been reiterated in no uncertain terms by Pope Francis, both orally and then in his book interview for *The Strength of Vocation*. In response to questions by the interviewer regarding his views on the presence of homosexuals in the clergy, Pope Francis's words fully confirm the continuum between his papacy and that of his predecessor.

> It's something that worries me, because perhaps at some point it has not been dealt with well. Always on the line of what we were saying, I would say that in training we must take great care of human and affective maturity. [...] That of homosexuality is a very serious matter, which must be discerned adequately from the beginning with the candidates, if this is the case. We have to be demanding. In our societies it even seems that homosexuality is fashionable and that mentality, in some way, also influences the life of the Church. I had a somewhat scandalized bishop here who told me that he had found out that in his diocese, a very large diocese, there were several homosexual priests and that he had to deal with all that, intervening, above all, in the formation process, to form a different group of clergy. It's a reality we can't deny. There is no lack of cases in the consecrated life either. A religious told me that, on a canonical visit to one of the provinces in his congregation, he was surprised. He saw that there were good young students and even some already

professed religious who were gay. He wondered if it were an issue and asked me if there was something wrong with that. Ultimately it's not 'that serious, it's just an expression of an affection'. *That's a mistake. It is not just an expression of affection. In the consecrated life and in the priestly life there is no place for this kind of affection. For this reason, the Church recommends that people with this rooted tendency are not accepted in the ministry or in the consecrated life.* The ministry or the consecrated life are not their place. Priests, religious men and women religious should be urged to live celibacy in full and, above all, to be perfectly responsible, trying not to create scandal in their communities or in the holy faithful people of God by living a double life. It is better that they leave the ministry or the consecrated life rather than live a double life. [My italics]

Thus far, then, the official line, the doctrine with its robust and uncompromising condemnation of homosexuality and total exclusion from the priesthood of all homosexuals, including those with a 'genuine' vocation willing to abide by the lifelong chastity requirement. In other words, homosexuality should in itself be sufficient grounds for exclusion from the seminaries even when not 'practised', i.e. total celibacy.

The real situation is a very different one. In this and the huge majority of cases the sociological reality is a world away from the official line. And seminary trainers are all too aware of this. Tricou (2019, p. 13) reported an honest assessment by one of these, a 60-year-old priest, who noted that

> Not one [of the trainers] believes this rhetoric, at least, not in the seminaries. However, I've been a member of two training teams, in two seminaries, and I can talk about [X] Seminary that I also know quite well, and I think you can also say the same for [Y] Seminary, so that makes four seminaries, er…and more widely, because we regularly have meetings with other seminary training tutors. So, no one believes these things! No one! And everyone has always thought that hunting down gays in the clergy was pointless, at least everyone apart from fundamentalists, schemers, sycophants, and repressed homosexuals.

Let us begin by saying that the Church's attitude to homosexuality is effectively a profound and deeply rooted ambivalence, a disconcerting double speak. With massive hypocrisy, Catholicism condemns homosexuality whilst at the same time fostering the conditions in which it can best flourish (Jordan 2000, p. 7).

In fact, the doctrinal terms used to describe homosexuality are often parodies, with it often being portrayed as a disease. Adopting a rhetoric borrowed from 19th century positivism, all Vatican documents and interviews with popes make a distinction between 'transitory' and 'permanent' homosexuality, as we have seen, namely between 'curable' and 'incurable' forms. Certain scholars (Jordan 2000, p. 28) have gone as far as to argue that the primary purpose of the whole Catholic sexual ethics framework, and especially its exaltation of procreative sex, is to combat homosexuality.[2] In this interpretation the central importance of the heterosexual family in Catholic doctrine is little more than a pretext for its real purpose – punishing gays. To ensure that homosexuality does not harm humanity, spawning disaster, violence, destruction and death, Jordan argues, the Church sees homosexuals as needing to be isolated and silenced, reduced to total political impotence. The duty of gays wanting salvation and to remain within the fold of the Holy Mother Church is thus to avoid sex and scandal, i.e. to hide their shameful sexual orientation. Gays are thus required, first and foremost, to keep well away from the priesthood, and not to try to become priests. All official documents take it for granted that homosexuals are external to Catholicism, treating them as if they were all naturally residents of the world but not of the Church, a sort of alien and strange people, a race apart to be managed by 'the bride of Christ'. Homosexuals are frequently blamed by the Church for the sex scandals which have erupted across the world in recent decades: for many priests, clerical paedophilia is quite simply the outcome of clerical homosexuality. Accusations of deceitful behaviour – and of having formed a lobby – levelled against homosexuals are frequent in Vatican circles and used as a weapon against internal enemies. Pope Francis has used this strategy against his enemies and these latter have done the same to him.[3]

The Church, which condemns homosexuality in public, has always warmly welcomed a great many gays into its ranks, however. This is tangible at all levels, especially at the apex of the Church hierarchy. As Martel (2019, p. 10) has written, 'Homosexuality spreads the closer one gets to the holy of holies, there are more and more homosexuals as one rises through the Catholic hierarchy. In the College of Cardinals and at the Vatican, the preferential selection process is said to be perfected, homosexuality becomes the rule, heterosexuality the exception.' An expert on the clerical world and himself a priest, Donald Cozzens (2006) has even gone as far as to ask whether the clergy may be becoming a 'gay profession'.

Mandatory celibacy is undoubtedly a way of avoiding questions being asked about priests' sexuality and thus very frequently of covering up homosexuality. Jordan (2000, pp. 118–119) noted that many popes have been gay and that a great many documents have condemned the presence of gay priests and their sexual activity. To cite one of the best-known works, Peter Damian's 11th century *Liber Gomorrhianus* railed against 'networks of sodomite priests' who absolved one another after sexual relations and 'incestuous families' of actively homosexual priests and bishops (Jordan 2000). Protestants have long accused Catholic parishes and monasteries of being dens of homosexuality (Jordan 2000, p. 133). Male friendship is constantly extolled in the clerical world, including in the lives of saints, on a par with misogyny and revulsion of women.

Even in its punishment of homosexuality the Church has always been more tolerant than the civil authorities, frequently denying the latter the right to charge members of the clergy accused of sexual crimes, including right up to our own day. More generally, many features of clerical culture overlap with gay culture, i.e. its mannerisms, actions, styles and clothing. In this context, so pervasive is homosexuality in the clergy that it might be said to define the very way of being and doing of all its members, including heterosexuals (Jordan 2000). Once again according to Jordan, if heterosexual culture expects all males to behave as if they were straight, the clerical world expects all priests, including heterosexual ones, to behave as if they were gay. The priest stereotype is packed with traits uncompromisingly rejected by traditional heterosexual culture, with the blessing of the ecclesiastical authorities – examples being a fixation with aesthetics, effeminacy, sensitivity, delicacy, excess and hysteria. A passion for cassocks, ornaments and regalia are a further ever-present distinguishing feature of homosexuality in the clergy, while disputes around liturgical elements between the exponents of informality and devotees of tradition and formalism echo those between the various components of the homosexual milieu, argues Jordan (2000).[4]

Jordan (2000, p. 161) also added that Catholic seminaries, especially the most conservative ones, are one of the few places in modern society in which homosexuality is experienced traditionally, namely covertly and a world away from the logic of 'coming out'. Reporting the results of his enquiry, Martel (2019, p. 7) notes the attraction homosexual priests admit to feeling for the sacraments, the tabernacle, the double curtain, the ciborium and the monstrance.

> There's the magic of the confessional, toll booths rendered fantastical by the promises attached to them. The processions, the recollections, the banners. The robe of lights as well, the vestments, the cassock, the alb, the stole. The desire to penetrate the secret of the sacristies. And then the music: the sung vespers, the men's voices and the sonority of the organ.

Lastly I would add that even the Church's radical and universal opposition to civil rights for gay couples can, from this perspective, be considered a symptom of the authentic and profound bond existing between the clergy and homosexuality: what the Church fears most is that gay emancipation might jeopardise the recruitment of homosexuals into the Catholic priesthood which has always sheltered and defended them. For Tricou (2018, p. 3) the basis of the clerical battle against what is known as 'gender theory'[5] is the same. In this sense the Vatican's battle against homosexuality in the clergy could be seen as none other than a masquerade, a smoke screen designed to hide a truth which is as denied as it is real.

There is also plenty of empirical evidence of homosexuality in the clergy in a range of social research, both recent and otherwise. For example, just under 50% of the sample marshalled in James Wolf's important 1989 research consisting of over 100 cases were gay and this number was even higher amongst the sample's seminarians, at 55%. It was still higher amongst the youngest in the sample, at 60%. The 50 homosexual priests interviewed by Wagner (1981) reported a disconcertingly huge number of sexual partners – 226 – a frequency of at least two sexual encounters per week. On the strength of a sample of almost 3,000 cases accumulated over many decades observing and assisting the clergy beginning in the 1960s, Richard Sipe (2013) estimated a percentage of gay priests at around 30%, whilst acknowledging that this figure had soared in recent generations to the extent that a figure of 75% might now be considered credible. Over 40% of the priests contacted by Hoge and Wenger (2003, p. 102) believed that there was a gay subculture in their seminaries, with this figure rising to 46% for the younger members of the clergy, the under 35s.

In a more recent work, Kappler, Hancock and Plante 2013, over two thirds (exactly 67%) of the priests interviewed were gay, with 5.8% being bisexual and only 26.9% straight.

More generally, despite the absence of the sophisticated methodological tools available today and without specifying sexual orientation, former 16th century priest Martin Luther considered just one in a thousand priests capable of keeping their celibacy vows (Qirko 2001, p. 66; Phipps 2004, p. 153). A further well-known habitué of the Catholic ecclesiastical milieu, Swiss reformer John Calvin, came up with a similar estimate in approximately the same period, adding an incontrovertible quality judgement on this, writing that: 'Disgraceful lust rages amongst them, so then hardly one in ten lives chastely and in monasteries, the least of the evil is ordinary fornication' (Phipps 2004, p. 157).

Celibacy has always been a fiction.

Notes

1 https://www.vatican.va/roman_curia/congregations/ccatheduc/documents/rc_con_ccatheduc_doc_20051104_istruzione_en.html
2 For a critical analysis of Catholic doctrine on sexuality and relationships, see Turina (2013).
3 For Pope Francis see, for example, an edited version of the meeting with a delegation of South American monks and nuns on 6 June 2013 in the Vatican. For his opponents see in particular the accusations made of Bergoglio in the summer of 2018 in a detailed dossier by apostolic nuncio to the USA, Monsignor Viganò.
4 Jordan (2000, p. 195) wrote that 'the loud quarrels that continue to swirl around these changes have been presented as an aesthetic choice between Mystery, Tradition, Conservatism and Honesty, Innovation, Liberalism. You could favor complexity, ornament, and elegance or simplicity, bare passion and informality. Figured this way, the liturgical styles wars following Vatican II paralleled the quarrels between the assimilationist "homophile" movement and the radical "gay liberation". Both can be understood as competitions between gay styles.'
5 In point 56 of the *Amoris Laetitia* apostolic exhortation, Pope Francis states that gender theory is a dangerous ideology which 'envisages a society without sexual differences, thereby eliminating the anthropological basis of the family. This ideology leads to educational programmes and legislative enactments that promote a personal identity and emotional intimacy radically separated from the biological

difference between male and female. Consequently, human identity becomes the choice of the individual, one which can also change over time. It is a source of concern that some ideologies of this sort, which seek to respond to what are at times understandable aspirations, manage to assert themselves as absolute and unquestionable, even dictating how children should be raised. It needs to be emphasized that biological sex and the socio-cultural role of sex (gender) can be distinguished but not separated. [...] Let us not fall into the sin of trying to replace the Creator. We are creatures, and not omnipotent. Creation is prior to us and must be received as a gift. At the same time, we are called to protect our humanity, and this means, in the first place, accepting it and respecting it as it was created.'

10 Homosexuality in the Seminaries – Pain, Denial and Cynicism

Where secondary adjustments in the seminaries are concerned homosexual activity is somewhere in the middle of universally practised masturbation and the exclusion of sexual relations with women. In other words whilst masturbation is generalised and sex with women very rare indeed, gay sex is extremely commonplace – less prevalent than masturbation but more common than straight sex.

I believe that many actively gay seminarians feel shame and guilt about their sex lives, as in the case of Carlo, the protagonist of the story I told at the beginning of Chapter Three. I am equally aware that homosexual theology students include a number of 'cynics' who do not appear to be overly troubled by moral scruples. In an interview with Frédéric Martel (2019, p. 401), former gay priest Francesco Lepore went as far as to say that the fact that 'seminaries have a large majority of young gays has become quite banal: they experience their homosexuality as perfectly normal, and go out discreetly to gay clubs without too much difficulty'. For Lepore, then, the number of 'cynics' and 'opportunists' has increased significantly in recent generations, as has seminarians use of gay bars.

The availability of smartphones, social networks and chats has greatly increased the opportunities for priests to live double, triple, even quadruple lives in our era. All the same, I have significant doubts about the universal applicability of Lepore's affirmation to Italy as a whole, first and foremost because the greater social acceptability of homosexuality now permits young gays to be open about their sexuality to a much greater extent than in the past. Why should they then feel that priesthood is the only way open to them, with the systematic and risky double life which comes along with it? Why would they choose lies and secrecy when such a sexual orientation is less and less a source of marginalisation, social isolation and professional discrimination in society at large. It is thus, in my opinion, still highly likely that the young homosexuals opting for the priesthood are, for the most part, men who 'do not accept their sexuality' and for whom it is a source of malaise, guilt and denial. Secondly, whilst there is no doubt that the opportunities for gay sex have soared, thanks to social networks, apps and night clubs, it is, however, equally true that seminarians' freedom of movement is

DOI: 10.4324/9781003426271-10

still extremely limited as, on average, they are allowed to leave the seminaries only once a week to see their families and visit their parishes. The openings to go to bars and meet people is thus fairly limited. I would thus be tempted to limit the validity of Lepore's statements on the proliferation of 'cynics', for the above reasons, to those parts of the country – essentially rural areas and southern Italy in particular – where homosexuality is less accepted and where decent well paid jobs are much more difficult to come by. But in such areas gay clubs are few and far between.

Ultimately I believe that the situation Lepore describes is true primarily of Rome, a city lacking neither in gay bars nor seminarians coming from rural areas and a long way away from home. In general terms, I believe that the situation described by Drewermann (1995) 50 years ago still applies. The German theologian believed that Catholic clerics are not, at least initially, lacking in good will and willingness to work hard but that it is only when they are urged by the Church to see their true value in their clerical status alone that they are fully ready to do all that is asked of them.

In any case I will begin this analysis from the obverse of this cynical type, namely from 'problematic' gays, those who are uncertain about, or struggle to accept, what they are afraid might be their sexual orientation, of whom there are a great many in the seminaries. Such men remain entirely celibate for some time for this very reason, including in the seminaries, obviously not without frequent significant suffering and pain. This view of mine is confirmed by Father Arthur, one of the gay priests contacted by Tricou (2019, p. 9): 'In fact, the more the church has developed a homophobic rhetoric, the more it has attracted homosexuals who were in denial, at least at the beginning of their careers.'

For example, when a teacher at elementary school asked him what future career he had in mind Father Giuliano instinctively answered 'priest, Miss'. 'I've always been attracted by holiness and spirituality, fascinated by silence and interested in meditation', he said.

> I was a sensitive, affectionate child. I joined a minor seminary at the age of fourteen, after a vocational meeting which was truly an inspiration for me. I knew I was attracted to boys when I was as young as seven or eight. I was aware that I wasn't much interested in girls. But for many years I was so focused on getting ready for the priesthood, on spiritual training, that I blotted out all thoughts of relationships. Solitary sex was all I did, with an immense sense of guilt. At a certain point, however, my sexual fantasies began to increase, as did my attraction for my fellow seminarians. I spoke to my spiritual father about this and he told me not to worry, that it was normal, that I certainly wasn't the only one in this difficult situation. He reassured me in a fatherly way. He didn't judge me nor, above all, threaten to have me thrown out of the seminary, but he certainly was of no help whatsoever in dealing with the problem. And no-one else I asked helped me either, starting with the rector. At the seminary, sex was a total taboo.

Homosexuality was certainly not a problem, as long as it wasn't discussed, that you didn't try to talk about it or do something silly, such as what I'm going to tell you about in a moment. In the meantime my fantasies grew and, at a certain point, I fell madly in love with a fellow seminarian, a heterosexual boy who later left the seminary. When he said goodbye it broke my heart, I was desperate. At that point, though, I wanted to understand, and I asked to see a psychologist. I was told it was impossible, that I would have to make do with spiritual direction, that there was no need for a therapist. So I started looking around, covertly, finding out more. I got some books which I read in secret, in my room at night. The trigger was the sudden expulsion of a fellow seminarian who disappeared overnight. Our superiors summoned us a few days later to tell us. They beat about the bush ridiculously and never touched on the salient fact: homosexuality. But they got across to us that we must have no contact whatsoever with this fellow seminarian for any reason at all. At that point I rebelled and told the rector and my spiritual father that I would see him anyway. And that's what I did and I found out the reason for his expulsion: he had been seen wandering around at an open air prostitution site. I was just about to be ordained and all hell broke loose. A mobbing campaign was started by fellow seminarians and superiors. I was told to go home to my parents' house. I was told that this would give both me and the church the opportunity to think about the step I was about to take. Ultimately I was definitively expelled, told that I was not suited to the priesthood and could try again a few years later. I was saved by a person I met at a spirituality week, an older man. We became friends and then lovers. It was my first time. I was 27. In the meantime I began seeing a psychologist, who was an enormous help to me, as he helped me understand the meaning and terrible consequences of the violent sexual repression I had suffered. Finally I found a northern Italian bishop, also homosexual, who ordained me in the end.

In some cases the gratifications of seminary life and an unconscious desire to deny the truth of one's sexual orientation contributed to putting seminarians off from dealing with emotional matters. This was true of Father Giuliano and also of Father Giuseppe, a boy from a not-especially religious working class family who stopped going to church soon after confirmation, like many other boys of his age. During his national service in the 1980s Giuseppe met a follower of a church movement, attended a few prayer meetings and converted right away, thinking that this was his opportunity to make sense of his life and turn it in a joyful and meaningful direction finally. At one of these group meetings Giuseppe met a girl and embarked on a relationship which lasted three and a half years, exactly the time it took him to take the decision to go into a monastery and become a priest. In this period the couple had sexual relations, though not full ones, for religious reasons they told themselves at the time, because they both wanted to remain virgins. But the relationship gradually fizzled out and came to a final end when Giuseppe decided to go into the seminary. 'I have to say', he confided to me years later and after protracted therapy,

> that I was never really much attracted to girls. I've never been repelled by women but I went out with them out of duty more than anything really, because it felt like the right thing to do. In any event, during the three years we were together something happened which, at least momentarily, increased my suspicions, the question marks over my sexual identity. It happened during a trip to the lake. Our group was staying at a monastery and a brother there showed great interest in me, a great desire to get to know me better and find out more about me. At a certain point we ended up on our own in a secluded room at the monastery and had oral sex. He did everything. I froze, as if I was paralysed, shocked at what was happening. For me it was like psychological violence, close to rape, made possible by my ingenuity. After the shock of the first few days I tried to forget the whole thing, to dismiss it as a moment of weakness, not truly important, nothing to worry about. I joined a monastery a few months later and from that moment on my passion for God began to take up all my energies. I didn't even masturbate anymore and considered my many night time ejaculations as simply a matter of biology. I didn't feel the need for sex, because I saw sexual activity as bound up with relationships and so if I wasn't in a relationship, I said to myself, I didn't need to have sex. And if one day I had problems on this score, I thought God would help me. I was so innocent Marco! It took dramatic events in later years and dozens of therapy sessions before I realised that I'd understood absolutely nothing about me and men.

Let's move on now to the stories of those who had sex in the seminaries, beginning with men like Father Valerio, who, just like Carlo in the story we've just seen, learnt the basics about sex in the seminary. He joined the seminary as an adult, at around twenty-five years of age after graduating from university and it was only then that he fully grasped his sexual orientation.

'Look', he said at a certain point of our long interview in his parish presbytery,

> the seminary environment is so steeped in homosexuality that it's certainly a great place to become gay. I had an inkling that I was 'different', that I wasn't attracted to women. I'd had girlfriends but we hadn't done anything physical and I hadn't at the time wanted to get up to much. I strongly suspected that I was attracted to men only but the problem was that not a single one of my group of 'old' friends, my school mates and university friends, boys from my street, was openly gay. I expected to find the same state of affairs at the seminary, but I couldn't have been more wrong: I realised right away that the seminary was packed with gays! In general things

there went as they did between me and Michele, my first partner, a year older than me. There weren't many of us in our group because mine was a small diocese. Michele and I made friends right away. It was easy for him, because he already knew what he was doing, and wanted to get me into bed. One evening we were in his room, sitting on the bed, and he put his hand on my knee. It started out as a game and we quickly ended up having sex. The first time in my life! It was, as I soon found out, 'priestly' sex, i.e. no feelings, just a physical act, exclusively carnal and genital. We never hugged or kissed. There was no tenderness, we didn't even cuddle in the years we had sex. Michele, the future Father Michele, now vicar general to the bishop at my diocese and likely future bishop, never talked about what we were doing. He tried to avoid all reference to this 'thing'. This felt monstrous to me. I wanted to understand. It certainly wasn't just a game to me. It wasn't just a matter of sexual pleasure and orgasm, but something much more profound and important. Something I had inside me and that the context I lived in had helped me to deny for a very long time. One day I told him outright: 'Let's tell it as it is, Michele. We're gay.' 'Speak for yourself', he answered harshly, 'I'm definitely not gay.' I think he was totally afraid of himself, of accepting his homosexuality. It's said that he now suffers from frequent panic attacks. It doesn't surprise me because I believe that he is totally subsumed by his role and, so to speak, 'totally out of touch with himself', that he has given up all forms of authenticity and leads a fake, double life. In any event, at least at the beginning, I was so shocked that I felt the need to turn to my spiritual father. I told him about it and asked him if he didn't think it would be best for everyone, both me and the Church, that I leave the seminary right away, as homosexuality – and even more so practising homosexuality – was significant grounds for expulsion from the Catholic priesthood, if the Vatican documents were to be believed. He gazed at me in understanding and told me not to be hasty, that what had happened to me was 'normal', that I could still be a good priest after finding this out and that what was important was that I pray a lot and try to control myself, that I trust to the Virgin Mary and try hard and constantly not to fall prey to temptation. So he reassured me and convinced me to remain at the seminary. Ultimately no-one took my suffering seriously, no-one helped me to cope with my homosexuality. No-one really looked after me, beyond platitudes and truisms. But I am quite sure that all my superiors were themselves gay. The most ridiculous thing is that they all seemed most concerned with keeping seminarians away from women. As if that was the problem! Nothing could have been simpler than keeping women at arm's length for that band of homosexuals that was us at the seminary.

Naturally, as we have seen, not all gay seminarians are as innocent as Father Valerio when they enter the seminaries. Others have had plenty of experience with the pleasures of the flesh and are thus perfectly well aware of their sexual orientation. As we have seen, the availability of social networks and

Homosexuality in the Seminaries 67

the challenges inherent in superiors' attempts to control internet use at the seminaries have made engaging in active sex lives immeasurably easier for seminarians, both inside and outside the seminaries.

In some cases, above all relatively 'unmodern' peripheral areas, choosing opportunistically to go into the priesthood to hide one's sexual orientation is essentially the result of realising that one is gay. 'Now, after years of therapy, I can admit without too much suffering', says Father Lorenzo, a young priest in a remote southern Italian province,

> that it was the lack of other job openings and, above all, the fact that as a homosexual I couldn't have found a better place to live, that prompted me to go into the seminary. I've certainly always been very religious and had a passion for all things holy, for liturgy, processions, popular devotion, but the truth is primarily that I didn't want to emigrate, to go to Milan, I didn't want to leave my hometown. And, as a gay man I didn't want the double life that many southern Italian men lead. It was a priest who convinced me to join the seminary. He told me that seminarians were once straight when they went in and gay when they came out. The seminary broke them in. Now they're all gay right from the start. I joined at the major seminary, in theology. Sex was easy because we were in single rooms, but the bathrooms were external and all you needed to do was to make a date in there for a quickie. We covered each other's backs, knowing that no-one was going to get themselves into trouble by reporting themselves. In fact you could count the heterosexuals on the fingers of one hand, including amongst the trainers, starting with the rector. Identifying potential lovers was very easy. You just used your 'gaydar', the gay radar. Inside and outside the seminary. Like the year I went to bed with a deacon in the year before his ordination as a priest. He came to my town for the ordination of another boy. I accompanied him to the presbytery. The way he looked at me was unmistakeable and he massaged my hand. We exchanged phone numbers and met for sex a few days later. In general, another priest and gay man told me that there were once more priests and it was easy for them to find a partner within the clergy. Today, fewer priestly vocations means that you have to look outside and this, unless you pay an escort, increases the risks of being found out a lot. And so of getting into trouble. Because, above all for a seminarian, the main problem is not getting found out, causing a scandal, showing that you're unreliable, that you can't guarantee that you know how to avoid jeopardising your image and, above all, that of your organisation.

The words of a seminarian interviewed by Martel (2019, pp. 413–414) meld Father Valerio's doubts and Father Lorenzo's cynicism:

> […] the seminary was primarily a temporary solution. I wanted to see if homosexuality was a lasting thing for me. Afterwards, the seminary

became a compromise solution. My parents want to believe that I'm not a homosexual; they like the fact that I'm in the seminary. And in a way it lets me live according to my tastes. It isn't easy, but it's better that way. If you have any doubts about your sexuality, if you don't want people around you to know you're gay, if you don't want to hurt your mother: then you go to the seminary! To return to my own reasons, the predominant one is clearly homosexuality, even if I wasn't originally completely aware of it. I only really had confirmation of my homosexuality once I entered the seminary. I think it's a kind of rule: a large majority of priests have discovered that they were attracted by boys in the homo-erotic and strictly masculine universe of the seminaries. When you're at your school in the Italian provinces, you have only a very small chance of meeting homosexuals that you like. It's always quite risky. And then you get to Rome, to the seminary, and there are almost only boys, and almost everyone is homosexual, and young, and handsome.

In some cases priests justify the lying in the name of a quiet life and protecting the reputation of the institution in churchgoers' eyes. We might explain their behaviour in terms of cowardice and opportunism, as well as implicit disparagement of lay people, as the following Tricou interview excerpts clearly show (2018, p. 10): 'I could not leave the church', a diocesan priest said to the French sociologist.

> I had my boyfriend, some colleagues knew that. However, I had never sought to put him on display nor to demand that he have an official position, because it was out of the question that I could harm the church with this story. Another priest revealed: 'Listen, you had to be discreet, even if it wasn't easy. You couldn't flaunt your sexual plight in public. First, because you're not just about your sexuality, and also because when a priest speaks, he speaks not only for himself, he speaks for the church, an institution that is already sufficiently weakened. And then there are the people of God, the parishioners, what would they say? They wouldn't have understood. And if they had understood, I'm not sure that shocking them would have served any purpose. Quite the reverse.

Another of my interviewees, Father Angelo, told me that:

> It was an emotional bond with a priest which pushed me in the direction of theological studies. It was my parish priest, who was ill when I was in the fourth year of high school. I thought, then, that if I had been a priest too I would have been able to help. Once I joined the diocesan seminary I had lots of lovers, but all of them outside the institution. I took every opportunity for casual sex with partners I met by chance, in some public place, in parks, on trains, buses, streets, anywhere, but not in gay bars.

I've never been to those. In any case I didn't trust my fellow seminarians, even though it was obvious that the vast majority of them were gay too. I was afraid that they might blackmail me. At the beginning I told my spiritual father at least some of what I was doing and suffered from guilt. Then I realised that I wasn't doing any harm, that I wasn't killing anyone, that I wasn't having sex with children. I couldn't see why I shouldn't go into the priesthood. In any event, more or less half way through theology I was expelled from the diocesan seminary. I was desperate when I met the founder of a community of friars. He was brilliant at pulling the wool over my eyes, persuading me that the diocesan priesthood wasn't for me and I would love the community, that it was the best place for me, etc. So I joined. Almost right away I realised that it was a terrible place and that I was to be the object of the attentions and violence of the founder. He had sex with me all the time, as with all the other members of the community. He was jealous and possessive but didn't care about me in the least. He used me. As he did everyone. I didn't like it and the violence he inflicted on me caused me a great deal of suffering.

The few heterosexuals in the seminaries frequently lead entirely separate lives from the homosexuals, noting or at least guessing at what was going on, the sex, even if they didn't take part in it. There are exceptions to this rule, however, and sometimes, above all in the minor seminaries, the heterosexuals turn to the homosexuals for sex, 'in the absence of alternatives', we might say. This was true of Father Fulvio, who never doubted his heterosexual orientation. But there aren't any women in the seminaries. 'So you did what you could', he confessed.

Obviously I masturbated, but almost right away, and right through high school, I also had a few fellow seminarians masturbate me. They were gay and enjoyed masturbating the many fellow seminarians who were willing. We did it by night, in the beds of the dormitories we all slept in together. It was frequent, at least two or three times a week. One of the two was in love with me and wanted to touch me all the time. I never touched him and when he touched me I thought of the body of a girl in my home town who I really liked. In my dormitory, apart from the two masturbators I mentioned, there were two further boys who made their bodies available to the others, offering oral and anal sex. I had sex with them too but I liked this less. The anal sex in particular made me feel as if I was really gay. I knew it wasn't my thing. There were twenty of us in all in the room: four offered sex and the others took them up on it. There was always a certain ruckus at night. You could hear lots of bed-hopping. I think our superiors knew all about it but had no intention of interfering. What they feared most for us was girls. They were afraid that we might fall in love with a girl and give up the seminary. They knew all too well that homosexuality, lived discreetly, is not a problem for seminarians. All the same I felt hugely guilty. I was always thinking about how God would punish me for these failings. I used to think that God was looking on as I masturbated, or worse, when I let myself be touched or other things. Sometimes, in my imagination God looked like my father, a callous, unpleasant man who beat me for the slightest thing. In my head I was constantly begging for forgiveness, apologising obsessively, telling him that I was sorry for giving in to temptation, but that I just couldn't resist. I felt terribly guilty. I spoke to no-one about it. At confession I spoke only of masturbating.

But the consequences of the massive presence of homosexuals in the seminaries are much more subtle than this and go well beyond the opportunity for sex, including for heterosexuals. In this respect Father Carmine's revelations are very interesting, as a young heterosexual southern Italian priest:

When I joined the seminary I found a great deal of 'men dressed as women', boys who reminded me of the women in my family in their way of doing things and the attention they paid me. When I spoke to them it was like talking to my aunts. They had a terribly female vision of the world and were always noticing what I wore, telling me off when they noticed something which didn't match. In one of their bathrooms I once found a hand cream. In their rooms there were often flowered shrines of the patron saints of their hometowns. Before ordination they shaved their legs and chests as if they were going to a sex party. I must admit that there was something pleasant about this attitude of theirs which I would never previously have suspected. They made me feel like an alpha male. They were very caring with me. It was less competitive than the world outside, with the boys in my hometown. They knew I was never going to go to bed with them and respected that. You might say that they were like mothers to me. My mother was undoubtedly an interfering and domineering woman but also a very protective, affectionate, loving and attentive one. I was definitely dependent on her and not always in a healthy way, like when she forbade me from locking the bathroom door and broke in on me when I was in there. If they tried to seduce me it was subtle, confiding things in me and asking for my advice. One of them, for example, confessed to me that the sight of another seminarian's bum by chance excited him. He asked me anxiously whether I thought he might be gay, because after this he had masturbated fiercely. And, not realising that he was trying to seduce me, I took him seriously asking him if a girl's bottom had the same effect on him.

Homosexuality is sometimes seen by certain heterosexuals as a source of trouble and discrimination. This was the case of Father Mario when he was at the seminary:

In my seminary, and almost all others as I discovered, there was a full-blown gay lobby and a very widespread one because you could count the heterosexuals on the fingers of one hand, out of a total of 50 boys. There was even a dress code, and they all dressed and did their hair in the same way. And they had a great deal of sex with each other. One day the rector broke in on them during a threesome. They were expelled right away, but soon afterwards that rector was transferred elsewhere and those three boys came back. Now all three of them are rectors of minor seminaries. That rector's successor is now bishop and in turn super gay. We called him 'the Queen' for his overbearing manner and effeminacy. He was obsessed with body hair: following his orders we all had to be hairless. He loathed us having even a single hair on our faces. In any event it is important to remember that sex in these places was not only, or even primarily, a matter of enjoyment, of pleasure. There was more at stake: power. The point is that the gay lobby ruled the diocese. It decided who went where, enjoyed a plethora of privileges. Sex is a way of recruiting new members of the lobby. The sect's seminarians recruited others who were made new members. Being penetrated, for boys who are often virgins, is an initiation rite: it means being willing to be dominated, showing you're submissive and trustworthy. And complicit, because you were breaking a rule together which applied to both of you. A subtle urge to give in, to join the lobby to win power, to get promoted was pervasive in the seminary. You started by being appointed to get the liturgical celebrations ready, i.e. sacristan, liturgist, organ player, choir leader and, above all, master of ceremonies and then, once you were priest, moved on to posts of all sorts. The worst of all my superiors was the rector, famous for his 'hugs'. He clasped us to him, touched us all over and you felt his crotch very clearly. Then he stared at you to gauge whether you were resisting, whether you were trying to get away or would let him do what he wanted.

Systematic, non-fragmentary and anecdotal information about facts such as these are very hard to come by. The total secrecy and silence the Church requires of those living within it, its threats of terrible punishment, means that we can guess a great deal about what happens but know very little. The 2017 publication (in Italian in the Catholic journal *Il Regno*) of Brazilian research data on homosexuality in the seminaries (dos Santos and Guareschi 2019) caused a sensation. This is work which cannot be accused of bias, not only because it involved an anonymous questionnaire in accordance with social science methodological dictates, but also because it was published by *Revista eclesiástica brasileira* and, above all, because the researchers are themselves clergy at the Congregazione del Santissimo Redentore, as theologians and social psychologists (dos Santos and Guareschi), and had the full backing of the managers of the two Brazilian seminaries the data was gathered in. The results of the work strikingly substantiate the accounts outlined thus far in this book, and in a geographical context a long way away from Italy. Its authors wrote of the article that '[...] for seminarians homosexuality is a presence in the seminaries. For them homosexuality is commonplace and an increasingly frequent fact in the training institutions.' Some caution is required, however. 'The majority of the seminarians are homosexual but a certain discretion has to be kept up.' From the seminarians' point of view, homosexuality is not simply a fact but also a practice (dos Santos and Guareschi 2019, p. 5). The seminarians interviewed admitted that 'it is a delicate matter which is not always discussed or dealt with as it should be' (dos Santos and Guareschi 2019, p. 5).

The young aspirant priests interviewed believed that around 80 percent of seminarians actively sought out sexual partners, above all via 'communication groups' and they saw homosexuality in the seminaries as close to universal, around 90 percent. These young men are asking the Church to speak directly to homosexuals, accept their presence in the congregation and in the clergy. Some of them go as far as to say that homosexuality is not a problem to be solved but simply an undeniable fact. Many acknowledge that '[...] many young men are frightened of coming out as gay to society and their families' and that 'some homosexuals effectively see seminaries as a way out of having to take on the responsibilities bound up with heterosexual behaviours within the family and society' (dos Santos and Guareschi 2019, p. 7).

The future priests taking part in the research also noted that 'many seminarians realise they are gay when they are already in the seminaries, because they find certain conditions there which contribute to the development of homosexuality' (dos Santos and Guareschi 2019, p. 7).

For the Brazilian seminarians those responsible for them should 'help candidates take stock of their homosexuality' (dos Santos and Guareschi 2019, p. 7), guiding them and assisting them in every way possible, contrary to the current state of affairs.

In conclusion, what all the accounts reported imply is that homosexuality amongst young aspirant priests, as well as in the clergy itself, is categorically different from the Church's depiction of it and actually in no way problematical for the Catholic Church hierarchy. Quite the contrary, homosexual priests have always been seen as greatly preferable to heterosexuals by the institution as the former constitute a much lesser risk of scandal and abandonment of the priesthood than the latter. And, even more importantly, the stigmatising of homosexuality in Catholic doctrine has concretely consolidated the dependence on it of gay priests who have traditionally been more zealous, conservative, disciplined and orthodox than heterosexual priests, whether because of self-hating internalisation of homophobia or simply a need for the institution's protection (Schlegel 2013, cited in Tricou 2018, p. 8).

Two factors, at least, have changed this situation recently. The first is reduced deference to the Church amongst journalists and information providers that are now willing to lift the veil of secrecy which has long concealed the clergy's sexual and emotional lives, and are no longer fearful of the Church. The full truth about what happens in the seminaries is still very far from having come to light and we are still frequently dependent on anecdotes – a still limited number of stories and facts – but we certainly know more today than we did yesterday and much more than we did in the past when the Catholic sex taboo paralysed even the free press and the social sciences. We have already looked at the second of these two factors, the greater social acceptance of homosexuality, a sharp drop in the stigma attached to same sex attraction. The chance to live freely and openly as a homosexual is draining the clerical vocational pool because it reduces the proven attraction to the seminaries, unconscious or otherwise, felt by many gay men and fosters the abandonment of the clergy by homosexuals achieving relaxed acceptance of their sexual identity.

All the same – and whatever the doctrine might say – homosexuality remains a preferential state for recruitment into the Catholic clergy.

It is in the seminaries, to use Catholic doctrinal jargon, that the shift from transitory to permanent homosexuality most frequently occurs, within which individual homosexuality is acknowledged, consolidated and practised, and relatively low risk safe, silent and discreet coming out takes place.

As Jordan has written (2000, p. 170): the '[s]eminary is often the first place where young gay men can encounter a significant number of other gay men'. The seminary environment is so suffused with homophily that even heterosexuals sometimes experiment with 'situational homosexuality', as we have seen, and in general, gain a familiarity with 'gayness': '[...] all Catholic priests in America, gay or not, participate in one culture deeply colored by gay tastes and gay fantasies: the predominant clerical culture itself.' Ultimately,

> [...] for the last four centuries the increasingly centralised institutions of formation have been preoccupied with instilling and enforcing celibacy. At the same time as they isolated groups of young men from secular influence under an imitation of monastic life the institutions have created intensely homoerotic conditions. The 'seminary' or 'seed bed' was invented to enforce priestly discipline in the Counter Reformation. But its enclosure meant, inevitably, that the erotic temptations of the medieval religious houses were now offered to most candidates for the diocesan priesthood as well.
>
> (Jordan 2000, pp. 141–142)

Thus it has, above all, been heterosexual priests who have been discouraged from joining the priesthood, as 'shame and guilt of an isolated homosexual encounter were presumed to be [by the Catholic hierarchy] positively motivational rather than deterrent to celibacy' (Sipe 2003, p. 134).

The leaning towards homophily and homosexuality is decisive right from the moment of recruitment. For Sipe (2003, p. 149) the fact that the Church favours the recruitment of teenagers whom it directs to the minor seminaries is to be explained by the fact that adolescence is the 'necessarily homosexual phase' of development, 'when male idealisation is high and sexual activity more childlike than adult'. Living in an entirely male environment favours the extension of this state ad libitum for many seminarians.

As we have seen, seminarians discover these and other profound institutional 'cultural assumptions' gradually, a little at a time, and often never take full stock of them (Schein 2010). Such assumptions belong to a sphere we might call the collective unconscious in which an organisation's members obey and consolidate these in their everyday practices, but sometimes unconsciously and without them ever being transformed into objects of explicit socialisation.

In any event, for many homosexual seminarians, the path to self-discovery and acceptance is invariably a solitary and extremely troubled one which moves step by step with their equally lonely and painful realisation of the way the institution works. This latter is led to a considerable extent by gays who have, in turn, travelled this same challenging path and witness the evolution of their successors from afar with an eye primarily on generating loyal and effective future functionaries.

The sole, and only apparently paradoxical, effect of the restrictive policies set in motion in recent years (which I referred to in greater depth at the beginning of chapter nine) has been to reinforce this tendency to consign boys discovering their sexual identities to the shadows, to secrecy and solitude. This may be a deliberate policy by those managing the Church, designed to recruit functionaries capable of employing homophobic rhetoric whilst, at the same time, being increasingly careful to hypocritically mask their own true identities, in the face of the terrifying challenges to the Church deriving from growing social acceptance of homosexuality and reduced media deference to clerical culture.

11 Rare Birds in the Seminaries
The Challenging Lives of Heterosexual Students

For most of the few heterosexual seminarians, women are an alien and mystifying race. When they join the priesthood many heterosexual seminarians are still virgins in every sense of the word, having had no sexual experience of any sort whatsoever with women. Naturally, as we will see, it is precisely the physical absence of women – with the exception of a few elderly cooks or cleaning women – that almost invariably places them centre-stage in the everyday fantasies and romantic dreams of young heterosexual seminarians. It is the lack of contact with girls which is behind their greatest frustrations, the primary conscious and unconscious cause of unhappiness. An institution which, as I have attempted to show, is extremely tolerant where homosexuality is concerned, makes absolutely no such concessions in its strict embargo on heterosexual sex. And this is understandable: a heterosexual relationship may be the first step on the road to a family life, taking theology students away from the seminaries and leading them to give up the clerical life. This is a serious failure for the institution, potentially involving the loss of a future priest and bringing an expensive and, in some cases, lengthy investment in the training of such future officials to a distressing end. It is only after ordination that seminarians enjoy virtually total sexual freedom and their chances of leading active emotional and sex lives increase exponentially.

In any event, the sex-phobic seminary context transforms even the most innocent sexual and emotional urges into grave sins, converting everyday situations into circumstances to be hidden. The repression which comes with this inevitably brings sex to the centre of young seminarians' thoughts.

For example Father Giovanni tells of having joined a small southern Italian minor seminary at the age of fourteen. 'Right from the outset', he remembers,

> everyone told me that I must go nowhere near girls under any circumstances whatsoever, that I had to keep away. My father told me that if he heard that I was seeing someone he would 'punch my lights out'. The result of this was me feeling marginalised, different. I grasped that I was no longer one of the crowd, I was predestined, a special, already adult person. My boyhood had quite suddenly come to an end. When I went

DOI: 10.4324/9781003426271-11

back to my hometown I had to wear a cassock and surplice and everyone called me 'our little Father Giovanni'. I was sixteen when I fell in love for the first time. It lasted close to a year. The object of my love was a girl in my parish. We never even kissed. The only time we were seen together in the town square, chatting, it was immediately reported to our families and the parish priest, who gave me quite a dressing down. We developed our own sign language to communicate with. I remember that we once happened to be on the same bus to the regional capital city, me to go to the seminary, she to go to the convent boarding school she lived in. We certainly couldn't sit next to one another but we gazed at one another with understanding and desire from a distance. One day I secretly gave her a cheap ring. It was the most important moment in our brief and imaginary love story. Her name was Rosanna. I still remember today that during mass, unnoticed, I replaced the Hosanna with her name, shouting out 'Rosanna in the highest!'

During his seminary years Giovanni had other, entirely virtual fantasy platonic romances. He told his spiritual father about all of these, also mentioning the possibility of giving up his seminary studies, and the latter invariably responded that it was an excellent sign that his was 'an authentic vocation'. 'These words rang in my ears day and night', he still remembers angrily.

I didn't get it: there I was telling that priest, my spiritual father, the explicit reason for my suffering, I mean a desire for women, and instead of telling me, as I expected and, deep down, hoped – as I didn't have the courage to take the decision on my own – that I had to leave the seminary, he urged me to see it as positive for my priestly vocation. It was ridiculous! At a certain point I stopped talking to him about it. I just couldn't stand hearing those words anymore! I continued to feel like a sinner, totally unworthy of the priesthood, a blasphemer incapable of loving Jesus with the same huge love he gave me. There were other loves, all platonic, and I kept going in this way right to the end, until the Ignatian weeks [prior to ordination] during which I came out with all the details of what was torturing me, what I'd done wrong. It was a huge liberation, one of the few occasions in which I finally felt pure and innocent, ready to take on the priestly life which I shortly embarked on. But it was just a hiatus. Most of the time I was permanently plagued with inner conflict: on one hand I felt strongly attracted to the priesthood, on the other I felt totally unworthy of it. And this as a result of my constant longing for a girlfriend, to kiss, fall in love with and make love to. The most incredible thing for me then was that this conflict was viewed entirely differently by the Church, as an unequivocal sign of the authenticity of my vocation. I just couldn't get a hold on this. I even tried, just before the Ignatian weeks to be seen in public with a girl in the hope of being caught and sent away. But it didn't work!

When they do happen, seminarians' first sexual experiences are replete with guilt and secrecy, impossible to talk about, covert and inevitably disappointing. The impossibility of a free relationship prompts some to resort to paid sex with prostitutes. This was the case of the then 23-year-old Giacomo who decided, in the summer of his third year of theology, that the time had come to explore new worlds, to travel around Europe. He asked a fellow seminarian to go with him on this trip. 'I asked him to come', he says,

> because I was too scared to go alone. It was my first time abroad. I had no idea what I was doing because I was used to living in an institution which did everything for me. In the seminary I didn't have to decide anything on my own, I couldn't do anything on my own initiative. So I asked this friend to come with me, even though I didn't trust him fully. You can't trust anyone in the seminaries. You are always scared that your fellow seminarians might betray you, report on you, show you up, perhaps for some selfish reason, to show off to our superiors, be false friends, Judas. The climate was one of constant terrible suspicion. A perennial fear of being thrown out. So I never confided my 'sins' to anyone, which were essentially masturbation because nothing else was possible at the time. My companions did not confide in me either and so, in my total ingenuity I imagined that I was the only sinner around, that the others were all virtuous and in any case better than me. So off we went. It was August. Our first stop was Budapest and we ended up in a red light bar of the lowest sort where we watched a strip show in a sort of dark underground den together with a few other people. When the show ended two of the girls who'd performed on stage came up to us and suggested we went upstairs with them. We agreed and were taken to a dark room with bunk beds in it. We separated. I climbed up onto the upper bunk and saw a naked woman for the first time. I was over twenty at the time. I was so excited that I had an orgasm almost immediately, as soon as the girl touched me. When we left the bar, in accordance with the 'code of silence' we'd learnt at the seminary, we said nothing to one another, not a single a word about what had just happened. I think what had just happened was his first contact with a woman too. In any case I never asked him how it had been for him and he didn't ask me either. We never spoke about how it had felt, nothing. Not then. Not ever. In the days that followed we behaved as if it had been a day like any other, as if we'd gone to a pub. This was our way of telling each other that our respective secrets were safe, that we would never speak about what had happened on that bunk bed.
>
> We continued our journey to Amsterdam. There, in the red light district, I finally had sex for the first time with a large blond girl. If that's the right way to describe it. It lasted something like thirty seconds. And on this occasion, too, I didn't say a word to my friend. We returned to

the seminary and never spoke about our experiences. I didn't make love again for at least four more years and was ordained priest in the meantime. This was the beginning of a period of deep suffering for me, however. I spent many night time hours watching porn films. I got up late in the morning, skiving off prayers and often school too. I started not turning up for exams and became a priest a year late in the end.

When urges for sex and love come more insistently to the fore in seminarians' lives they can, at least in the early years of training – those marked by idealism and guilt – lead to very painful tensions. If they are kept at bay and resisted in some way they generate feelings of triumphant heroism in inexperienced seminarians, a thrilling feeling of belonging to a superior species of being capable of controlling their feelings and passions.

This was the case of Father Ferdinando who joined the seminary at the age of eighteen, as he now recalls,

> with huge idealistic zeal. I was attracted to the missionary life and exploits, I loved the idea of devoting my life to the poor and needy. Of taking the salvation message to them. I joined the seminary with this drive. And with great interest in theological studies, in liturgy and the scriptures. Then, during my third year of theology studies, I met Luisa and fell suddenly and desperately in love. She was my age and I found her very beautiful and intelligent, irresistible. Our interests were the same, both of us were spiritual and theology enthusiasts. We read and meditated on the Gospels and other religious texts together. We began meeting up on Sundays when we went home. First in public places and then, despite our best intentions of remaining celibate, on our own, in the country, in cars, at home when her parents were away. We ended up having a sexual relationship, though not a full-blown one. Our desire for one another got stronger and stronger. My soul was increasingly on the boil and I was plagued with terribly conflicting feelings: on one hand the deep love I felt for Luisa, on the other an equally powerful desire to be a priest, to make a dream I'd had since childhood come true, to answer that call from God which I felt so strongly. They were two vocations which I felt with equally dramatic intensity. I cooked up ridiculous excuses for myself to temper the searing pain of this contradiction. For example I often thought that it was not right to simply smother my feelings for Luisa, that it would be wonderful if I could turn it into a chaste friendship. 'All' I needed to do was to drive out the idea of sexuality and exclusivity. On one hand I told myself all this, reassuring myself that I could do it, but then when I saw her I realised that my desire for her was getting stronger. And I felt angst to the point of tears at the idea that she might meet someone else, fall in love with some fellow university student. That would have killed me. In the end, to get away from her, and already a priest, I had to go all the way to Africa.

Sometimes desire is too strong for expression and repressing it generates symptoms requiring psychological attention. This was the case of Father Dario, who grew up in a family of fundamentalist Catholics, with a domineering mother who was interfering, possessive and authoritarian.

> It took twenty years of therapy to get it out and come to terms with it, to accept the fact that I joined the seminary as a result of the huge pressure exerted by my mother and because I could no longer stand living with her. I began at the minor seminary, in the first year of middle school, when the seminary felt like an escape from home. And in the end I never left and went into the priesthood. Obviously the main reason for my distress was the absence of women, the lack of significant relationships with girls. It was a terrible amputation for me, above all on the emotional and loving plane. The idea that I would never be loved terrified and depressed me, although at the time I had no concrete prospect of meeting women. In fact, how could I possibly have met anyone in that entirely male world and with my mother watching over every second of the time I spent outside the institution? I also had what, for me, were a few unimportant homosexual experiences: for a while I masturbated in the same room as a fellow seminarian. But that was just sex, although for a while I was literally terrified by the idea that I might be gay. It was the psychological therapy which helped me to understand that I am entirely heterosexual and that I was actually always thinking of women, of their love, which I missed so much. When I expressed my fears to my spiritual father or the family priest I was invariably told that it was all up to me, that I would have to decide which was the most important, women or the seminary, vocation or marriage. 'What is women's place in your life, Dario?' This is what my spiritual guides asked me constantly. And I suffered because I wanted both, because I never truly understood why they conflicted. I love Christ deeply, I really love being a priest, looking after people's problems, helping them to improve their lives and I adore theological debate. But like all human beings I want to be loved.
> In the end I never left the seminary but I started showing signs of deep rooted, radical malaise. I couldn't sleep, for example. In the dormitory all we minor seminarians slept in, in my personal cubicle, night after night went by with my eyes wide open and I had to go to the prefect's room to find relief and rest. He had a single room and let me take my mattress there, put it on the floor and sleep on it for a few hours. It was the only time I managed to get a bit of shut eye. I also got extremely aggressive with my fellow seminarians. I treated them badly and kept going on about leaving the seminary. When my parents or superiors were there, however, I usually kept quiet about this. I couldn't get the consequences out of my mind and this sent a shiver down my spine. Later, at the age of 18, when I was still at the minor seminary, I started smoking, first in secret and always compulsively, even as much as three packets a

day, a fatal addiction which had repercussions on my whole life. I even decided that I couldn't go to the Congo, where I had always dreamt of going, because it would be difficult to find tobacco there. There is no doubt that I was an addict but for me smoking was also a bid for freedom, something of my own, something different from what the seminary forced us to do. So, a rebellious, liberational act. A habit which made me feel less different from people outside, those normal people to whose ranks I unfortunately did not belong.

This 'forced diversity' following on from the decision to join a seminary is a recurring feature in priests' stories and one of the greatest sources of suffering in their personal stories. This is the case of Father Stefano, for example, who told of having joined the seminary of his own free will on the basis of a fascination, as far back as the fifth year of elementary school, with a deputy parish priest who was highly active and enterprising in the packed parish church of his town in the Lombard plains. 'I joined at middle school', he told me.

I dreamt of a priest's life spent doing good and passing my time with lots of young people. Right from the outset, however, I suffered from the fact that, as a seminarian, I was unfortunately already cast in the role of someone who couldn't do certain things. For example, I couldn't do what my friends were doing, I mean, do everything I could to take home a girl I like on Saturday evenings and spend time alone with her. If I did I was assailed with the most terrible feelings of guilt. At the seminary I was told that I had to identify totally with Jesus Christ and my peers in the parish no longer saw me as one of them, but as 'different', a seminarian, a half priest. I was perennially conflicted and riven with desire and conflicting urges. On one hand I realised that at the seminary I would have experiences (such as attending a classics high school) that would absolutely not have been open to me if I stayed at home with my parents. I knew that it would be wonderful to be a priest, that I could have a wonderful life devoting myself to others and to Jesus Christ. But on the other not being able to be a normal person, like everyone else, one of the crowd, caused me huge suffering. Someone who could enjoy being looked at by girls without feelings of inadequacy immediately afterwards. The happiness I felt at such moments led almost instantly to guilt, the feeling that I was a fraud, a bad person. I understood very well as such times that the main reason behind my 'diversity' in my own eyes and those of others was my celibacy, the universal expectation that I would not have sex. And I was effectively celibate in my seminary days. I expected to remain so my whole life. I truly believed, as did many of my fellow seminarians, that if I gave in to the temptations of the flesh I would be betraying God's trust. For years I didn't even masturbate, succeeding in resisting the provocation of one of my best friends who exalted the virtues of onanism. I knew it would be an extremely painful process as I liked and was attracted to women. We boys talked often about sex, about how big or hard our penises were, of those pictures in porn magazines which did the rounds of the dormitories.

If I think back to those years now, what comes to mind is feelings of inadequacy, a constant sense of failure, both as a man and as a priest. As a man I was a disaster because I'd never seduced a woman, as a priest I felt a failure because I continued to desire women and, from a certain point, I also masturbated. The year I graduated I fell in love for the first time. It was reciprocal. We spoke about it and started writing to each other regularly. I started thinking about leaving the seminary but I didn't have the courage and after a few years of platonic love she told me she thought that my true vocation was the priesthood.

I asked Stefano if he had ever had homosexual sex in the seminary. He said 'no', that no-one had made a pass at him either, although he could now see, years later, that some of his fellow seminarians and superiors were sexually attracted to him and that the vast majority of his former companions were gay.

No more than one third of the total in the seminary were heterosexuals. And in general the rule was the same as in the army: 'Don't ask don't tell.' Even if something happened, what was important to our superiors was that it wasn't mentioned. At all cost. Every now and again someone disappeared but we all pretended not to notice and no-one ever explained the reasons for these sudden disappearances. Going back to my attempts to lead a normal life, I tried very hard to keep up friendships with girls and was horrified by the misogynist priest cliché. In the seminary I kept well away from that large group of fellow seminarians who hated women and competed to heap insults and scorn on them. One of them – now a big shot in the apostolic nunciature, the Vatican diplomatic service – boasted of having insulted one on a train, of having called her an 'ugly witch', senile hag, a bitch. Everyone around him loved it, laughing and clapping at the story.

12 The Elephant in the Room
Secrets, Denial and Lies in the Training of the Catholic Clergy

> For centuries authors with various stances on Christian culture have taken for granted that lots of priests and monks are sexually attracted to men or boys and sexually active with them. They have also argued that the primary characteristic of clerical desire and sexuality is secrecy. In fact the single most common element in this work, both serious and facetious, is that the clergy takes a great deal of effort into keeping its sexual secrets. The medieval satirists poked fun at the clergy, arguing that priests pass more time covering up their sexual trysts than saving souls. Contemporary polemicists accuse the Catholic Church of being a gigantic machine with which to cover up terrible things.
>
> (Jordan 2000, pp. 136–137)

What real life and sociological analysis justification is there for the hypothesis referred to by Jordan here? Is the Catholic Church really bent on covering up the evil it itself does?

Answering to this question involves drawing conclusions from what we have seen thus far on clerical training which, at least since the Council of Trent, has been a full-blown extension of the ecclesiastical hierarchy (Sipe 2003). It also means putting forward a few hypotheses.

Let us start by looking at one of the facts that has come out of this work thus far, that seminarians are very frequently fragile, insecure boys fearful of failure, often tragically uncertain of their sexual orientations or clearly attracted to people of their own sex and terrified of the consequences of this. The Church is a safe haven for all these people, offering a solid, secure professional trajectory with a great many benefits and high social status attached. What the Church expects in return is total loyalty, unquestioning obedience.

It is in the seminaries that the obedience to the Church is inculcated, forged into the minds and bodies of its young functionaries by means of discipline, radical dependence and the eradication of all space for personal autonomy. There is no room for rivals in this bond. It is inherently absolute and totalising.

Alongside discipline and theology, in their years of training at the Catholic institutes future priests also gradually learn how to manage their sexuality.

DOI: 10.4324/9781003426271-12

The first thing they learn is that publicly their lives must be epitomised by chastity, total self-control and explicit rejection of all forms of sexual pleasure, that they must, for the good of the institution – and thus for their own good within the institution – present as asexual and totally uninterested in the pleasures of the flesh. Breaking this rule, behaving differently or even simply formulating explicit doubts on the validity of the rules governing the sexual and emotional lives of the clergy means 'causing a scandal', i.e. blackening the institution's name, leading to immediate and forcible expulsion from it. Seminarians understand all too well that the institution can appear holy in the eyes of the world only as long as it is made up of holy men capable of giving up the foremost of pleasures to serve it, becoming 'eunuchs for the heavenly kingdom'.

Seminarians learn that sex must never be spoken of publicly, that it is only to be mentioned in private, in confidential conversations with fellow seminarians and, naturally, in confession and with their spiritual fathers. Officially, sex must not exist. 'Men of God' must appear to be capable of doing without, and anyone incapable of projecting a chaste image is unworthy of the status of elect. Within the seminaries, then, sex and love are the elephant in the room, something whose presence it is impossible not to be aware of but which everyone pretends not to see. This elephant is so huge that it dominates the scene but everyone pretends it isn't there (Zerubavel 2006).

Those with the best view of the elephant are clearly teachers, spiritual guides, educators, spiritual fathers, i.e. the adults who live and spend time in the seminaries. These men have coexisted with the elephant since they themselves joined a seminary and their years of experience mean they are very familiar with it. They know every inch of its body, can predict what it will do and know its needs all too well. New recruits find out about the elephant a little at a time and it is often a bewildering and painful process.

What future priests gradually apprehend is thus that the most serious failing for the system they are part of is undoubtedly being caught out breaking the Church's codes of sexual or emotional conduct or being honest about them, publicly admitting their most intimate desires, with having sex and falling in love in the forefront. In other words, through a subtle initiation process young apprentice priests learn that silence and denial are the cornerstones of clerical culture and all their actions and social interactions must be inspired by them. Reactions to this vary: some fail to conform, explicitly rejecting these values and giving up their priesthood ambitions, while others make 'secondary adjustments', with varying degrees of success, in an attempt to carve out decent lives for themselves without giving the institution up. On one hand, this recourse to secondary adjustments is an inevitable and 'healthy' component in the character development of future priests, obviating total suppression of their personalities in the name of the demands and functions of their role. It is, however, on the other hand, the premise for the emergence of generalised and callous cynicism, a propensity to consider morality a purely formal and public matter. Having had the same experience themselves in the past, seminary managers are very familiar with the clumsy exploits of their charges and turn a benevolent blind eye to them, like adults watching toddlers learn to crawl. The system thus crystallises and reproduces itself over and over again.

In purely organisational terms it cannot be denied that silence and denial play an important part in seminary life, generating social integration and group solidarity and forestalling the embarrassment and shame involved in dealing with matters seen as delicate. Ignoring, glossing over and pretending not to see something obvious are thus in some ways powerfully cooperative acts serving to maintain high social group cohesion: the elephant is there in the room but everyone is having a cup of tea as if nothing out of the ordinary is happening. Everyone present is thus, from that moment on, complicit in this pretence, this huge collective and individual lie, simultaneously liars and witnesses to the lies of others. Blackmailable and blackmailers at the same time, both potential victims and potential accusers.

Everything directly or indirectly relating to the elephant is steeped in silence and secrecy in the seminaries, with a generalised 'conspiracy of silence' (Glaser and Strauss 1965). When someone is expelled from a seminary no explanation is given and the other subservient recruits never dare ask for one. The reprobate's place is cleared away immediately and the traitor replaced by another apprentice – in deafening, all-round silence.

Over time this silence and denial are inevitably fortified (Zerubavel 2006), and habit forming for individual seminarians; they become mental habits, lifestyles and behaviours. The huge number of people caught up in this lying consolidates the overall mechanism: the more liars there are the lower the moral and cognitive price these pay individually for their immense collective lie and thus the more sustainable it is.

Silence and denial undoubtedly facilitate seminary managers in their organisational attempts to stave off rebellion, as seminarians each believe, in their silence-reinforced innocence, that they are the only sinners in a world of saints. If sex was talked about freely and explicitly, all the aspiring priests would find out that masturbation is common practice in the seminaries in the same way that sexual desires and fantasies are common and "normal" and homosexuality widespread. If sex were talked of openly it would be impossible for the organisation to maintain its control over seminarians' lives and manipulate them via constant individual blaming.

Total silence on the subject of sex and feelings blocks the development of critical thought patterns, of mature autonomous intelligence, and this too is positive for those managing the seminaries and the hierarchy as a whole. Just like in the universe of Orwell's *1984*, the absence of words, of a framework within which to formulate them, blocks critical thought, castrating the imagination and human freedom.

Lastly, once again on the subject of positive consequences for the institution, mass silence and denial make *omertà* towards the outside world on what happens within the seminaries possible, enabling anyone – journalists or scholars – attempting to reveal the truth to be accused of having made up the whole thing, of being mad or at best partial or distorted.

Ultimately silence and denial safeguard the total institution from prying eyes, from unwelcome public democratic attention. But their consequences for society and the Church – in the sense of God's people – are extremely negative.

A rigorously imposed 'culture of secrecy' encompassing the most unmentionable of crimes, namely sexual abuse, generates an organisational climate in which reciprocal suspicion rules and no-one can fully trust the others. Where systematic hypocrisy is the rule people spend most of their time wondering if they are at risk of being reported, what lies behind other people's words and what motives might lurk behind the actions of their peers. It is a world ruled by fear, by whistleblowing, by the universal diffidence reigning in the seminaries. Within them everyone knows, or learns over time, that no-one is telling the truth, to doubt and protect themselves from their fellows.

The outcome of an organisational regime such as this is profound collective immorality. The inhabitants of a world like this gradually come to the realisation that alongside the official truth lies another unconfessable one and that surviving the system involves not taking the former too seriously whilst following the latter to the letter.

13 A Free for All
The Sex Lives of Heterosexual Priests

Once ordained, the lives of men choosing a career in the priesthood change diametrically. Whilst as seminarians they are constantly watched over, treated like children, subjected to military-style discipline and forced into constant self-abnegation (Goffman 1961), as priests they enjoy extremely wide freedom of movement. Whilst as seminarians they are obliged to live in groups at all times and spend minimal time on their own, as priests the people they mix with are the much less interfering and pervasive parishioners. They experience what Sipe (2003, p. 82) referred to as full-blown 'psychological mode shift'.

Their clerical careers generally begin as assistant priests and continue at varied speeds – depending on the pastoral qualities demonstrated, the availability of posts in their diocese and other miscellaneous factors – in the direction of appointment as parish priests. Parish priests are their own masters. In their parishes they make all the important decisions, live with whoever they want (sometimes even their families but generally alone) and occasionally with fellow priests, and have a great deal of free time. Certainly, Damocles' sword in the form of intervention by the bishop hangs over their everyday lives at all times – perhaps following on from a letter from some parishioner, sometimes even malicious in intent, or even the sudden transfer to a parish high up in a remote mountainous region. But the risk is relatively small, even virtually non-existent, if young parish priests make use of the virtues of prudence and pretence learnt, as we have seen, with such sacrifice over the course of their long seminary years. Anyone forgetting these will need to be ready for hell fire and brimstone. As happened to the priest interviewed by Anderson (2005, p. 80), who suddenly (and imprudently) decided to come out as gay and was thus subjected to strict supervision, deprived of his freedom of movement and subjected to 6 o'clock curfew at the institution hosting him. This was his bitter conclusion: 'When my honesty and sexual integrity were not declared, I was given major responsibilities for administration and finance as well as great freedom. Now that I have been honest and adult, I'm being punished, treated like an irresponsible boy.'

In general, in Sipe's opinion (2003, p. 50), no more than 2% of priests live in 'perfect' and irreversible celibacy and a further 8% get very close. He does not, however, explore the bond between this state and priest age, i.e. we learn nothing of the average age of those belonging to this minority of priests capable of abiding by the rules.

For heterosexuals this 'free' life often means discovering women and sex. And it is not only a matter of the opportunities parish life offers for contact with women. Other elements are decisive, too, such as an end to community life and all that comes with it (significant reduction in social control, but also the pleasures bound up with the ultra-intense sociality which living in a peer group entails) and the downward spiral of youthful idealism: the bitter realisation that the institution they once so admired and venerated has serious shortcomings and is ultimately no different from other human institutions, for both good and ill. Distance from their seminary companions generates loneliness and isolation; idealistic disillusionment then leads to cynicism and sometimes resentment of a Church institution which ultimately asked much more of them than it gave. When they leave the seminaries a great many priests feel quite literally deserted by an organisation which had, until then, looked after every single detail of their lives. As a 40-something parish priest of a small town just outside Turin told me years ago: 'The bishop forgot all about me. If the locals here started worshipping goats, it would be of no interest to His excellency. Perhaps he wouldn't even hear of it.' The terrible certainty that they have lost the affection of their superiors feels unmistakeably like betrayal to a great many priests and it is a sensation which lasts for quite some time, even their whole lives.

In any event, both states – solitude and cynicism – prompt members of the clergy to seek 'compensation' of various kinds, from football to alcoholism, by way of money, travel and social media addictions. And a great deal else. Top of the list of these compensations is naturally sex and love, sometimes together, sometimes separately. In contrast to assumptions deriving from homophobic stereotypes, heterosexuals are no less sexually active than homosexuals (McGlone 2002), as my own data also clearly shows. For example, the former Father Alberto told me of a first, for him world-shaking, sexual experience right after ordination.

> I was assistant priest in a small provincial town. I met a girl of about 35, a catechist and the wife of a parishioner, mother to a child of first communion age. She was nine years older than me and started coming to my home increasingly frequently. One day she asked if she could use the bathroom and came back out in her bra and pants. She said she wanted to make love to me, that she was in love with me, that she hadn't been able to have sex with her husband since she met me. We ended up in bed. In the 15 months which followed I was swept away with passion. I finally discovered the pleasure a woman's body can give you. I never truly fell in love but soon became addicted to the sex. The relationship came to a natural end, you might say, as our passion gradually faded. The feelings of guilt which would have destroyed me a few years earlier were very

much tempered by my simultaneous discovery of the frequency of diocesan entanglements and trysts. My own lover also spent time in the diocese and told me that I shouldn't feel guilty about having sex with her as a great many of my fellow priests also had secret relationships. She told me stories of the personal secrets of a few priests. So my initial innocence faded very quickly and I began suspecting what soon became a certainty, that the Church maltreated all of us, all priests, that it used secrecy and silence to isolate us and make us feel guilty, to make us feel totally worthless in the eyes of God and the community. A little later I decided that the time had come to widen my cultural horizons and I enrolled at university, and a few years later I also started seeing a psychotherapist. I began to realise that the Church has nothing significant to say on anything that really matters. All the doctrine I had learnt at the seminary had intellectual appeal, aesthetic beauty, for me but over time I gradually realised that it was totally irrelevant to people's real problems. My appreciation of laypeople, non-priests, grew and I increasingly entrusted them with many of the parish's important posts and tasks. It was precisely in this context that I met my current companion. She is from the south of Italy and when I met her she had just left a violent, alcoholic husband. I'd seen many priests age terribly and die even worse, on their own. I wanted to avoid this fate.

The story described by the former Father Alberto is a recurrent one in the accounts I collected. One of the fullest and most interesting of these is Father Amedeo's.

The period just after ordination is a special one. The expression in our world is that priests are in 'a state of grace'. Our superiors had spoken of this at the seminary and after consecration I experienced it for myself. Incredible feelings of euphoria swept over me. I was able to confess for hours on end. I was the young priest and everyone, especially young men and women, came to get to know me, confess, invite me out. In confession I discovered that feelings of guilt were enormously widespread and invariably related to sex, sex and sex again. To tell the truth I felt some solidarity with penitents, because my problems were the same as theirs. I thought about sex all the time too. In this sense confessions were a very serious source of temptation, especially because it is, above all, women who go to confession, at least here in Italy. I remember a girl once, a very beautiful one too, telling me that she'd been to bed with two men. Like on other occasions I got very excited in the confessional, taking advantage of the fact that behind the grate and in the darkness I could see her but she couldn't see me. A few minutes later, as soon as I got the chance, I masturbated thinking of what I'd heard. When things like this happened I always thought how lucky my many homosexual fellow priests were in that they didn't get excited around women.

Another priest Father Franco remembered that

> at a certain point, a few months after ordination, the shyness I suffered so much from since childhood, my fears, all magically disappeared. I was idolised by the parishioners, a sort of demi-god. I so subsumed myself into the role of man of God that I grew a long Jesus-style beard. I'd been assistant priest for a few months when I met Elena during holy week. She'd been in an unhappy relationship for ten years. It was a relationship wanted by their families, her's and her partner's. She was 23 and a complete virgin, like me in fact. She came for confession a few times and then we decided to meet up outside. Our eyes met more and more often, we ended up kissing passionately and making love. We met at hotels a long way away from home. She was my great love, the only great love of my life. Thanks to her I discovered sex and women's bodies and experienced the immense pleasure involved. I've had many other relationships since but my heart still beats fast if I think of Elena.

At this point in our interview Father Franco asked to break off for a moment, as he felt overwhelmed by the feelings this memory brought up for him. When we started up again his tale continued thus:

> These were six months of hugely intense, all-consuming, absolute passion. She hoped I would leave the priesthood. She didn't say so in so many words but made it clear constantly, never stopped talking about it. Being with her, discovering carnal love, brought my priestly honeymoon to an end. I was upset and worried. At Sunday mass, she always sat in the front row, in front of the altar and gazed at me. Close by her boyfriend played the organ. I was desperate. I got the clear impression that everyone knew about our relationship, that my parishioners were aware of my lies. When I had to talk about faithfulness and conjugal love I felt terrible. I knew perfectly how hypocritical I was being. It wasn't a new feeling, as I'd felt the same sense of guilt every time I masturbated during my seminary years. I felt dirty, a sinner, unworthy of the gift of the priesthood. My relationship with Elena ended: the spell broke when I was moved to another parish, more than 50 km away. I never knew whether the bishop had found out about this affair and this was why he decided to move me elsewhere. In any case I was relieved. I wanted to remain a priest.

In his new parish Father Franco was soon a success with women. Soon after he arrived he went to visit the family of an elderly woman who'd just died and met the woman's granddaughter. After the funeral, the young woman went over to tell him that the words he'd used in his homily had moved and shaken her. After a few months of increasingly frequent meetings the two ended up in bed. 'Soon after the beginning of this relationship I met another woman', Father Franco continued, this time a young, sexually dissatisfied mother. It all began in confession when she described her frustrations. We got together when she came back from her holidays. When I saw her on that fatal day in September she was tanned and irresistibly attractive. She was wearing a mini dress which didn't leave much to the imagination. The guilt was even greater this time because of her children, who were regular visitors to the parish.

Father Marco's account fills in our picture further. He was ordained priest 15 years or so ago in a central Italian diocese and now manages an important Catholic school in his diocese.

'Leaving the seminary was something of a shock', he confessed.

You go from total surveillance, in which you have to ask permission even to buy a stamp, to the most complete freedom, responsibility for managing a parish or oratory, including its finances. Coming to my emotional life I can tell you that I was totally bowled over by a catechist younger than me, two months after I arrived in the parish. For reasons it would be complicated to explain here I was sent out of the diocese. This meant I felt more alone but also freer, less watched over by my superiors and my family. I was a total virgin and completely ignorant of sex. All I knew was masturbation. I'd never even kissed a woman. It was passionate. We ended up in bed almost immediately, although it was a while before we got much pleasure from it, because I was tragically unskilled. Our first times ended before penetration. In the end this girl became a friend and confidant for me. The feelings of guilt soon disappeared. I didn't repent of what I was doing. Quite the opposite. Having a partner finally made me feel like a normal person and also a happier and more complete priest. I found out that what would have been unthinkable to me just a short time before was quite possible: making love to a woman whilst remaining a priest. It lasted a year or so and ended because she wanted and asked for more. She wanted me all for her, that I leave the priesthood. Luckily she decided to do community service and wasn't around anymore. In any event the relationship changed my life completely. I discovered that it wasn't so difficult to seduce women, that when one of them was for some reason in crisis it was easy to take advantage, that many of them found priests sensitive, attentive and cultured and with a certain social reputation. I realised that even for a shy man like me, a bit dopey, goofy, there would be plenty of opportunities. In fact after this one I had many other relationships. A few years later I met Marta, a girl of my age I fell in love with. She was the type of woman I'd dreamed about in my seminary years. We began a nearly normal couple life made up of nights spent together, cruises and holidays. This went on for three or four years. At first I was drunk on the idea that I could have it all: the priesthood and a loving relationship, public status and private happiness. At a certain point, however, partly because of some tensions with the bishop, I started not being able to cope anymore. I asked her to live with me and told her I was ready to leave the priesthood. She replied that she didn't feel up to being judged by people, that we could go on as we were, that we could be happy even in this covert way. This was a huge blow for me. Thinking about it today I believe that it was for the best. It would have been simply to spite the bishop and my fellow priests, not a responsible, conscious decision.

In any case from then on I released the hand brake. I had myself transferred to another parish and had a succession of relationships. By then I had what you might call a 'modus operandi'. I began by discreetly paying them a bit of attention, confided in them and gradually built up a more intimate relationship. When we finally got together I'd put the brakes on, playing on my supposed feelings of guilt. I started saying that I didn't feel up to my priestly duties, that I didn't want to stop being a priest, that celibacy was important to me but that I had sexual needs that needed satisfying. I have to confess that I never really fell in love except perhaps with the first girl, the one I told you about. Naturally I was careful to choose the right women, weak people or semi-nuns who didn't know what they wanted from life. In one phase, those first years, my sex life was truly a mess; mine was a sex compulsion which led to me having many relationships on the go at the same time, even as many as five or six simultaneously. I still remember a community in which I managed to seduce all the female volunteers. I took my partners everywhere for sex: in pine forests in the midst of mosquitoes, in beech woods, at hotels. And I gave each one of them the impression that they were the only one, that it was exclusive. I didn't want to have to answer to anyone. Every now and then, at times of crisis, I spoke to some fellow priest about it. I was certain that they would keep it to themselves. They advised me to pray, to start from my ministry, to seek support in priestly brotherhood. But the most important thing, they all told me, was that you don't leave the priesthood. If you really can't do without, they advised, 'go and sow your wild oats outside your parish', meaning 'look for women a long way away from where you work'. It was precisely at this time that I enrolled at university and very soon graduated. My faith in the Church decreased day by day. I looked on in disgust at the institution's systematic trampling of human dignity in its attempts to protect itself. I saw the way paedophile priests and abusers were covered up. I'd come to a realisation that the institution's best servants were depressed priests or dirty, fat priests who'd let themselves go, who were no longer capable of seducing women and leading a life worthy of the name.

The ending to Father Carlo's story is different from the others and casts light on what can happen when priests' emotional lives get too complicated, especially when the institution takes action. It begins in the usual way, however. As a young priest Father Carlo was called to the home of a grieving family who'd suffered a terrible loss. At their house he also met 14-year-old Eleonora, an introverted, sensitive, very religious girl who volunteered at the parish. 'To tell the truth', Father Carlo recalled into my microphone,

> other girls came on to me but she was different, unique. I'd already had a few other relationships but I was really struck by Eleonora. I was 27 then. We exchanged phone numbers right away and started chatting on the phone every evening. We spoke about our day, confided our ups and downs. Those phone calls helped hugely with my loneliness, I felt comforted and reassured by them. We ended up in bed only much later, around a year and half later. I had other relationships on the go at the time but it was different with Eleonora right away. The tone of my sermons changed. I started praising love, not just conjugal love but also parental love, for babies. One day I made the terrible discovery that I'd got her pregnant. I'd never used a condom but had always got away with it until then. We were terrified and anxious about what to do. We were paralysed for weeks. We had no idea who to speak to. Right then the bishop wanted to move me to a large parish with many parishioners. It was an attractive prospect financially too, as I'd get lots of donations there. But I was broken. I was tempted to come clean about my situation. And to some extent I did. I went to a meeting of young priests and confessed that I wasn't praying any more, that I held mass only because I had to, out of duty. They were all very embarrassed. I'd dared to break the vow of silence which reigned supreme over priests' emotional lives. The bishop took me aside and told me that all I had to do was pray more, to get back the feeling that God loved me. I was tempted to run away. I stopped answering Eleonora's calls and left for Spain, where I stayed for over three months in a charismatic community. Its head, an Italian priest, suggested I remain there, that I throw my return ticket away and not return to Italy. In the end I went back to Italy and called Eleonora, who was naturally furious with me and also well on with her pregnancy. At this point I told the bishop everything. He told me not to worry, that I certainly wasn't the first priest to end up in this situation, that the Church would help me out. He suggested I leave Eleonora to her fate, compensating her monetarily or putting her into a care home which would look after her and her child. I dithered to begin with, frightened by the idea of leaving the priesthood, and agreed to spend a period of time at a home for priests in trouble. When I got there the director told me that he had already spoken to the bishop and knew all about my situation, that I would need to stay there a whole year, that I wouldn't even get to see my child, that they would deal with all the rest. They took my mobile phone off me and blocked all contact with the outside world. Then the daily brainwashing began, including telling me all sorts of terrifying scenarios. They told me that if I left the priesthood I'd have to work as a bricklayer, that I'd be a pariah, that I'd lose all the privileges

that go along with the priesthood. They showed me biographies of former priests, describing their sad lives. In the end I returned home and took a decision to leave the priesthood and marry Eleonora, ignoring the appeals of my parents and siblings who showered me with insults in the knowledge that they when I left the priesthood they would lose a good deal of money.

Clearly priests do not all have such frenetic sex lives. Some of them take decades to get over their fears and difficulties with women. Many of them end up, when they do give in and as a result of a certain underlying emotional immaturity, in being easy prey. An example is Father Alfonso, a central Italian priest, who told me he had had quite a few dalliances (always with girls in the Catholic milieu) for some time, but they were never physical and always turned into platonic friendships involving a great deal of praying together or remained little more than sweet talk, never full-blown sexual relationships. When these relationships came to an end Father Alfonso was distraught, and his repressed suffering frequently took psychosomatic turns. In one case, for example, when the girl he was in love with and had foreplay with told him she had decided to go into a convent, he ended up with all sorts of illnesses, from Legionnaire's disease to pneumonia by way of a worrying loss of weight. In the meantime he also, as assistant priest, had to fend off the attentions of his gay parish priest who confessed to having had an orgasm rubbing up against him on the bus and a few days later, with the connivance of the priest's housekeeper, left a G-string hanging on the door handle to his room.

During an interview lasting nearly three hours Father Alfonso reiterated that he had never had full-blown sex with a woman, adding that this would require him to fall in love, that for him sex and love had to go hand in hand. It was only when I had switched off the recorder and we were saying our goodbyes that he dropped his bombshell. He was insistent that he had other things to tell me, that he hadn't told me everything, that we would have to meet again and then, in a single breath, that he was no longer a virgin and that he'd had full-blown sex with a girl he'd met in Africa during a festival. He wore nothing identifying him as a priest and told no-one his real job. He'd met the woman he went to bed with just three times and would probably not see her again. Freeing himself of his obsession with love, Father Alfonso had finally succeeded in having sex!

14 Emotional Needs and Unbridled Sex
The Homosexual Clergy

For homosexuals, too, the transition to ordination and leaving the seminary constitutes a huge opportunity for a change in sexual habits, a new life. For those who had sex at the seminaries their new status gives them greater freedom to find new partners and attend Italy's various gay meeting places. The concern of the Church hierarchy is that such behaviour seriously jeopardises the institution's reputation. As in the case of Father Andrea, initiated into sex with men at his seminary and then, once he was parish priest, frequenter of gay saunas and bars.

'It was a whole new world for me', he said.

> I met lots of people and had a great deal of sex. But while I was excited by this new development I wasn't OK, I didn't feel stable. I started going to a psychologist. When my spiritual father found out, shortly before trying it on with me himself and then apologising for it, he told me to stop going, that I had to give up this 'shrink' stuff. He advised me to confide in a big shot in the diocese, who's now bishop. I never took this advice because I'd seen this priest once get out of a car in a gay cruising area. So not only was he gay but he was getting up to worse things than me! The truth is that they didn't want me to go to a psychologist because they were afraid that my story might get around. I remember that my spiritual father once asked me if I'd really told a woman my problems. The underlying message was 'Are you crazy? Surely you understand that you can't trust a woman? Can't you see that outside the ecclesiastical milieu there is no one whose reliability you can really trust?' In the end, when I got up to even worse, when I got together with someone who didn't accept my breaking up with him, who began writing to the bishop and anyone else he could think of, they handed me over to a priest psychologist they trusted and moved me to a new parish right away.

For another gay priest, Father Emanuele, it was online chats and the chance for 'anonymous' meet ups in cities a long way from his home parish which were determinant. He often gave a false name to people he met more than once and said he was a teacher. The only rule he set himself was not having sex with other priests. He wanted to be free at such times, he said, and not have to pile lie upon lie. But plenty of priests flirted with him and one even forced a kiss on him. Another put him up one summer in his parish and sent him covert messages from the pulpit during sermons, trying to convince him to have sex with him. Father Emanuele's problems began, as they did for many other priests, when he first fell in love.

> He was a great looking, attractive man, but what struck me most was his gentleness, the fact that he tried to take my hand in public, wanted us to go out to dinner together, for us to have a shared social life. I fell for him head over heels. One day I decided to tell him the truth, that I was a priest and when he heard this he left me on the spot. He said that he was horrified by the idea of being with a habitual liar like me and that he didn't want a life in the shadows, of denial and lies. I was shattered. I lost thirty kilos in weight and was all skin and bone. It was a former seminary professor who had left the priesthood who saved me. We met on the street one day by chance.
>
> He saw the pitiful state I was in, asked me what was going on and, when I told him, he said I absolutely must go to a therapist and that he knew a good one. I got absolutely no understanding from my fellow priests. They seemed scared by what was happening to me. The truth is that the church is a body which officially upholds heterosexual love, conjugal faithfulness, the family, etc. but in actual fact those working for it encourage 'emotion-free', compulsive, random sex. Because it is less risky for the institution, because it casts no doubt on the priest-institution bond.

Another gay priest, Father Alberto, described the consequences of his discovery of sex at the age of 28, after his ordination as a priest:

> Sex freed up energies I was keeping pent up inside, and helped me to grow, become a less angry person, a fuller and happier one. And more independent. Before I fell in love I was not very empathic with people, I was a bit arrogant, judgemental, presumptuous, always pointing the finger at someone, I felt superior to other people. Sex humanised me and gave me more fellow feeling, made me more human and better able to cope with the gossip that lots of people were saying about me. There came a time when my bishop realised I was gay and advised me not to go overboard, not to be too over the top, not to make a scandal.

Sometimes discovering sex and feelings requires a gradual maturing process for priests and many intermediate stages, including a few sudden revelations. This was the case for Father Alessio, long-term member of an ecclesiastical movement and equally long-term almost entirely celibate, for over 30 years. Father Alessio always suspected he might be gay but he'd never found the courage to admit it to himself. His first time came via the web when he signed up to a priests' chat group. In an exchange of messages a fellow priest told him of a 'religious homosexuals' group active in his town. When he heard this Father Alessio remembered dealing with the subject of pastoral care for gays during his theology studies. Without saying anything to his superiors, he thus decided to secretly join this group, to find out more, to talk, understand. The second watershed came soon after, one day, when he went by chance to a part of his town previously unknown to him with fellow priests and parishioners. That day Father Alessio was struck by the men he saw strolling around slowly, looking at one another and then stopping and starting walking again. It was clearly a cruising place for men. 'I remember', he recalls,

> the existential solitude their faces exuded. I decided to go back there to preach. When people came over to me I began speaking of Jesus Christ, the Gospels. A few men told me to 'fuck off' and I even got smacked a few times. That was how I met the man who was to be my lover for eight years, the love of my life. At the beginning the feelings of guilt were huge. A Jesuit father helped me enormously, telling me constantly that however much I might judge myself God was not judging me, that I had to move from what he called TUTP (terrible unconditional total protagonism) to TPA (terrible passive abandonment) – that is, I had to abandon myself to my relationship with God and this meant forsake myself. Looking back I realised that I'd been high on chastity but that, at the same time it had drained me of humanity. When I grasped that God loves me as I am it gave me a calmness I'd never experienced before.

A few years ago I acquired a copy of an extraordinary unpublished document where this book is concerned, Francesco Mangiacapra's 'gay priest dossier'. Although this had circulated widely in newsrooms and other media contexts and been seen by many people it had never, as far as I am aware at least, been subjected to systematic sociological enquiry. The reasons behind Mangiacapra's decision to compile the dossier do not fall within the scope of this analysis. All I will thus say here is that the declared purpose of the document was to foster moral renewal in the Church and its functionaries. 'The goal isn't to hurt the people I've mentioned', the first pages read, 'but to help them understand that their double life, however apparently convenient, isn't useful to them or to the people who rely on them for guidance'.

During one of the interviews he granted me, Mangiacapra told me that the dossier came about to some extent by chance, at the margins of his gay escort work. In his professional life Mangiacapra came across a priest who was much older than him and enjoyed and paid for his services. One evening this priest decided to introduce him to friends, a group of five men, all gay and all priests, in turn accompanied by a few 'friends'. Francesco was somewhat shocked, perhaps even scandalised and the idea of gathering information of this sort came to him. The next step was a simple one. Mangiacapra immediately linked up on Facebook with the priests he met that evening and this social network itself began suggesting other clerical friendships to him, setting in motion the conversations which made up the dossier. In this exchange of messages Mangiacapra acted as a sort of 'agent provocateur' in order to show what is normally hidden, namely the intentions, language and behaviour adopted by priests looking for sex. All the texts are authentic and their authenticity unequivocal, as are the photos of those featuring in the dialogues.

In gathering together his hundreds of pages of dossier, Mangiacapra was assisted by certain volunteers (two former seminarians in particular) who lent him their profiles and suggested further lines of enquiry, reporting names and, in a few cases, older conversations with priests and seminarians. Attempts to add new priests to the dossier then came to an end two months later, as the material collected in this short time period had already reached vast proportions. It is thus a small sample, limited to the gay clergy active on social media and dating-site chats in these parts of southern Italy. If just a few months of investigation could produce documentary evidence on more than 40 cases in a relatively small area (five or six southern Italian provinces), it implies that the overall scale of the phenomenon is much greater. I should also add that Mangiacapra told me that he had left out of the dossier the very few gay priests who turned out to be 'total beginners', innocent, not used to erotic conversations and clearly torn apart by doubts and feelings of guilt. These amounted to only three cases, however. The priests in the sample have thus all been sexually active for some time and are habitual users of gay networking apps, especially Grindr.

Once compiled, the dossier was sent to relevant bishops, many of whom – in line with a consolidated custom in the Catholic church and the vows of silence and denial which I have described in this book – simply transferred the priests in question to other dioceses without ever providing parishioners with the real reasons behind such transfers. The document shows that, in many cases, bishops already knew of the 'irregular' behaviour of some of the priests in the dossier from other reports. The impression given is that very few of the priests mentioned in the dossier got into serious public trouble as a result of it. A few were suspended and then reinstated, a few others promoted. Avoiding scandal at all costs is traditionally the primary goal of those at the apex of the ecclesiastical hierarchy. In fact, the names of the priests involved remained secret for the most part. Clearly we have no way of knowing whether and in what ways the priests concerned were secretly punished by their superiors or whether canonical disciplinary proceedings of some sort are under way. I believe that the dossier will turn out to be in some way one of a kind, as it seems likely that the many priests active in the 'sex market' will be more circumspect in their search for partners. Many of the priests present in the dossier have already taken their profiles off Facebook. In any event the dossier is an exceptional 'natural document' (i.e. one containing spontaneous conversations not generated for research purposes) of use to sociologists in their analyses of the private behaviours of members of the clergy.

The priests in question are almost all from the Campania or Lucania regions and concentrated in a few dioceses in them. A few seminarians and many other people are also mentioned in the priests' conversations as protagonists or as "prey" for other sexual encounters.

The priests are invariably either recently or very recently ordained and mainly aged from 30 to 40, the same age as Mangiacapra and the people who work with him and very probably the average age of those using Grindr. Others were expelled from seminaries in their youth and then let into others, allowing them to continue to ordination.

The more prudent of these, wanting to avoid leaving evidence that might constitute grounds for disciplinary action, use videochats and phone calls only or social media such as Telegram whose messages disappear automatically in a few seconds. All the others acted with impunity, taking no precautions whatsoever and seeming entirely unconcerned by their wide-ranging use of any means of communication. The issue of confidentiality is frequently raised and a generalised problem, however. One conversation defines priests who are known to have homosexual sex, i.e. those who make no attempts to cover up their sexual exploits, as 'faggots' and 'dangerous'. In general, many of them claim never to have had sex with laymen, much preferring sex with other priests, considered safer on a confidentiality level.

The content of the conversations is explicitly and exclusively erotic in nature and invariably accompanied by overt lewdness, in incredibly foul-mouthed language, referring to vast amounts of previous sex. They contain photos as well as videos of faces but also naked bodies, sex organs and the bottoms of young priests. And all of this in a range of poses and locations including, on one occasion, in front of a statue of the Virgin Mary. The dossier shows clearly that these young men take part in an easy-going, anonymous gay-sex subculture. Here and there the dossier contains references to gay meeting places such as bars and night clubs. The chats are fast-paced and voluminous, each consisting of hundreds of straight-to-the-point, obsessive messages whose sole subject is sex: 'passives' looking for 'actives', the size of sex organs, this or that sexual act. There are frequent references to group sex, often with other members of the clergy. In the event of 'first contacts' the passage from generic exchange of information to erotic messages is ultra rapid.

References to previous meetings and exploits are very frequent indeed and it is clear that the individuals involved have, in their recent pasts, from their seminary days or even before, had a staggering number of partners and that encounters are organised in nature, with full-blown networks of sexual partners made up of priests, seminarians and laymen. Every now and then the network fills up with muck, poison, threats and vendettas, furious revenge.

There are also a few bisexuals in the priest dossier. During a gay erotic chat one of them insists on being introduced to a female cousin or some other woman, for example. Another lives with his son.

Every now and then the priest's profession comes up in conversation: some 'services' needing to be performed, a wedding or funeral to preside over, Sunday donations accounts, spiritual exercises, a meeting with a young couple or the parents of a Sunday school child, a priest to be ordained in another diocese, followed by a night of sex and then back to the parish in the morning just in time to hold mass. Or a diocese conference, an excellent opportunity for a first covert meeting agreed in a chat, with details such as a hotel room door left half open and spasmodic night time expectation of a partner not yet met. We also know that the dossier's protagonists are at all levels in the hierarchy, occupying roles of various degrees of importance in the Church. There are parish priests, diocesan office directors and vice directors, sanctuary rectors, ecclesiastic assistants in the Catholic scouts (AGESCI).

Many meetings take place in the presbytery, generally in the evening. We also learn that 'professional' events such as journeys to assist at the ordination of a deacon from the diocese or a conference of diocesan bursars can turn into opportunities for sex. Some of the priests in the dossier even fantasise about employing a sexual partner as sacristan: 'I'd have you live with me so you'd be mine only.' And he adds: 'You'd do everything and sleep with me in the presbytery.'

There is even sometimes mockery of religious language, as in a chat commenting on a recent sex session in his bedroom at the presbytery in which a priest says to his lover: 'I couldn't not put you up. The Holy Father Benedict tells us that guests are Jesus Christ.' In another conversation a priest boasts in a chat that he was winked at by a young seminarian as he was crossing himself during the Eucharist.

The huge volume of messages in the dossier also include some from a priest under house arrest as he awaits trial (and then sentencing) for paedophilia, desperately trying to find partners willing to come and see him at his flat, as he himself cannot leave.

Paid sex is also very common (for confirmation of this see Martel 2019), as are fake identities, such as an elderly monsignor who pretends to be a wealthy diplomat with a private driver and contacts young gay men by telephone offering them work contracts or, more frequently, money for sex.

It must be admitted that there is a certain coherence in all this as these priests reject for themselves what they rail against at the altar, i.e. stable homosexual unions. They are effectively almost never looking for a stable partner, just casual sex, erotic play, 'random' and compulsive sex. The complicated business of conjugal faithfulness is left to the heterosexual couples they follow in their pastoral work.

On the other hand, they are fixated about clothing, cassocks, collars, body care and, more generally, appearance and image.

The 43 priests in the dossier speak of their very few heterosexual colleagues as 'black sheep', as rare isolated cases.

References to the seminaries and everyday life are frequent. A priest says to Mangiacapra pretending to be a seminarian that they're all 'faggots' (these are the words of the priest) in there and if he could return to the seminary 'there'd be a queue in front of his door'. Another priest admits that when he had sex at the seminary he put his mattress on the floor to make less noise.

15 Clerical Lies and Public Welfare

Our journey through the clerical universe – one of the modern world's least accessible and most obscure – ends here. It is, in many ways a relic of bygone days, an almost perfect plaster cast of our patriarchal and authoritarian past. Some might now say that it is, in a sense, at the end of the line (Diotallevi 2017). For others it is suffused with persistent, profound nostalgia nonetheless – with melancholic, intense and poignant longings.

Observing a total institution such as the Catholic Church deep down – the Church as a clerical institution and seat of power, naturally, not as 'God's people' or religious feeling – shows that within it nothing is as it seems and everything is diametrically opposite to what it seems on the surface. For example, from the outside it seems probable that the celibacy and chastity restrictions are bound up with sex, with a ban on sexual relations and emotional ties with other people. If this were the case we would view the sexual repression the Church solemnly decrees and puts into practice as highly important, in both good and ill. On closer examination, however, when we get down into the depths of its everyday life it is abundantly clear that sex has nothing to do with it, that it is not sex that is being repressed, but truth and authenticity.

As I have thoroughly documented, there is plenty of sex going on in the seminaries. Seminarians masturbate and have sex with one another, with their superiors and those outside the institution. Superiors bed their pupils, who in turn get one another into bed.

The institution's genuine fear is that its young functionaries will not learn how to keep what happens between the sheets hidden. It thus tries to ensure that they speak of it in detail only in the intimacy of confession (Foucault 2020), namely, only in such a way as to give the institution itself an insight into the stuff their apprentice priests are made of, into whether it is worth investing in them as 'men of God' or otherwise. Ultimately the only true effect of the 'ideological' repression of sex is to push it into the shadows, confine it to silence, surround it with secrecy and circumspection. The ban on sex itself is appearance alone, while the ban on speaking about it is substance, reality. It is the triumph of hypocrisy as the bond between speech and action (Brunsson 1989), as sophisticated tool of political governance.

DOI: 10.4324/9781003426271-15

As we have seen, this deeply rooted characteristic of clerical organisational culture is not immediately clear to novices (just as it is not clear to the large section of the population which still believes in the overall chastity and purity of the clergy). When they join the seminaries the vast majority of boys are innocent, as we have seen, inspired by great ideals and frequently more or less consciously afflicted by psychological problems of some sort, generally deep-rooted existential insecurities or a powerful desire to change or at least hide their sexual orientations (or both). All except the most cynical, 'seasoned' and opportunistic make the shift from self-blame and shame to acceptance of their sexual needs only gradually, adopting the hypocritical style of life so welcome, and functional to, the organisation, or they take action to leave the clergy or the seminaries. It is only after ordination that the primacy of secrecy and denial over chastity is definitively confirmed, however. After consecrating them, in fact, the institution might be said to let its young men loose into the outside world, making no further pretence at control over their lives or what they get up to. After watching scrupulously and obsessively over the personalities of its functionaries for years (in the case of those entering the minor seminaries, for over a decade) the institution now lets them go, entrusting them to pastoral work, granting them great autonomy, certainly significantly more than that normally enjoyed by bureaucratic functionaries. The private lives of new priests, their entire emotional and sexual lives, thus becomes an entirely personal matter from ordination onwards and the once all-pervasive ecclesiastical oversight vanishes altogether. They remain dependent on the institution only financially, above all on the strength of the fact that the training and skills acquired in the clerical world are extremely difficult to transfer to other spheres of life.

Naturally a great many young priests experience this change of attitude by the Church as a betrayal, an abandonment. The feeling of loss is that felt by ex-prisoners, former psychiatric hospital patients and those leaving the career armed forces, religious sects and the like. On one hand, as in the latter two, people's various motives for wanting institutionalisation encompass precisely the order and discipline it involves, a life with others and the sound education that goes with it. Non-voluntary institutions such as prisons and psychiatric hospitals can, on the other hand, feel caring and protective, with their clear rules making them feel safe. In any case leaving a total institution can lead to feelings of loss and distress, accompanied by overwhelming nostalgia. This is what many priests feel and it is this which explains high abandonment rates in the early years of priesthood and the emergence of other syndromes, from gambling addictions and alcoholism to compulsive pornography and unbridled sex. For many, leaving the seminaries is a trauma from which they never recover, an incurable wound which comes across well in the words of former Father Angelo, who joined a minor seminary at the age of 13, was ordained at the age of 26, left the priesthood at the age of 45 and is now a follower of another religion and a fierce critic of many aspects of Catholicism.

Everyone in my neighbourhood group of friends thought that just being in there made me essentially a total loser. But I considered myself super lucky. At the seminary we had opportunities which my friends outside it could only dream of. For example, we had film nights and could do wonderful sports. 'Do you have what we have?' I asked my 'lay' friends on Sundays, when I saw them and they looked at me in stunned silence. They couldn't even dream of the wonderful things we seminarians had!

'I come from a relatively poor family and there were opportunities in the seminaries which I certainly wouldn't otherwise have had' remembers Mauro, another former priest, from Lombardy, who joined a minor seminary at the age of fifteen. 'I was able to study classics in high school, play a great deal, meet interesting people I'm still in contact with. Overall in those years mine was a life of privilege as compared to those of people in my home town and social class.'

It is leaving the seminaries, the end of a life lived inside a total institution which is the main cause of 'clerical loneliness', not the lack of a spouse or family life. These are places which certainly do not foster men's human, emotional and moral development into adulthood. They are sealed up in a bubble, 'inside a condom' in the words of one of them, delaying their acquisition of 'adult skills', as compared to their peers, and of the resources needed for a relatively autonomous life. Many are aware of all this but the seminaries leave such an indelible mark on them that it never entirely fades and can sometimes re-emerge in dreams and an impossible desire to return to its protective womb.

In the same way as chastity and celibacy, the issue of sexual orientation also looks completely different if we get under the veneer. On the surface, we know, the Church explicitly and uncompromisingly condemns homosexuality and does everything it can to keep gays away from its bodies, especially the priesthood obviously. But in practice it is doing the exact opposite: offering hospitality and comfort to gays agreeing to live a life of concealment of their sexual orientation. The church provides a golden bridge for such people, enabling them to live in an entirely male world, which could not be more gay friendly, and to find lovers and partners with great ease, sometimes abusing their power and others' vulnerability, as in the cases we have seen, i.e. the rector who grabbed and forcibly clasped students to him and the spiritual director who performed overly meticulous nocturnal inspections in seminarians' rooms. It allows them to spend not a single minute of their clerical lives denying suspicions regarding their sexuality and to do so whilst passing for saints and hiding behind the convenient screen of celibacy.

In their training phase, as I have tried to show, life for heterosexual seminarians is much more complicated than that of their gay peers. After ordination the playing field levels out. At this point there is nothing the Church is not prepared to do to protect its functionaries, whatever their sexual preferences, including covering up defamatory accusations or, as we have seen, dealing with a child born from a priest's clandestine relationship and the parishioner who gave birth to it. So ordination marks a watershed in the balance of power between priests and institution they belong to, a turning point which works entirely to the advantage of the former. From this point on the decision to leave the clergy – with the exception of cases of serious crimes – can only be the result of a voluntary act, an autonomous decision by priests themselves.

I would like to conclude this book with a few considerations which have nothing to do with sociology, and especially the organisational analysis of total institutions, and more to do with social wellbeing and public happiness. The question I would like to start with is a very simple one: how important are the facts and interpretations which this book has brought to light and to whom? Beyond the right to study a subject such as this scientifically, who really cares whether priests are having sex or otherwise and what the purposes and consequences of seminary training might be? What importance does it have?

I have no doubt that the results of this work will be seen as biased and loaded by the majority of the more conservative and orthodox Catholics. This is the part of the Church and society which identifies completely with clerical culture, refuses to give it up and defends it tooth and nail, rejecting anything which does not endorse the optimal functioning of the clerical system and blame a few individual 'treasonous priests' for any faults in it.

For the progressive Catholic minority, on the other hand, which has been demanding the abolition of mandatory celibacy for years now, the book's arguments may be of use, if they agree to supplement their customary references to an era of Catholic history – in general terms the first millennium after Jesus's death when priests were allowed to marry – with radical sociological critiques of the current clerical system. The historical argument of a return to a married clergy is certainly crucial to the internal political and theological debate, but an empirical analysis of the current system might also contribute to calls for an immediate need for in-depth reform.

Alongside the conservatives and innovators, however, there is another segment of Catholicism and public opinion as a whole which would respond to the questions posed above by arguing that the culture of lies and secrecy which I have described in this book does not, at the end of the day, do much harm. According to this view priests having covert sex and emotional lives is not such a big deal if they are good pastors all the same, if they manage the community's heritage wisely, preach the Gospels effectively and follow both young people's education as well as families' spiritual lives with interest and care. It is, in fact, highly likely that some of the priests in the Mangiacapra dossier are able, for example, to separate off their public and priestly lives from their private ones completely and quasi schizophrenically, i.e. from private lives dominated by a 'regressive sexuality' guided by sexual play and made up of a host of furtive casual sexual relations in which, as Sipe has noted (2003, p. 153), 'maturity, judgement, and values lived and expressed in their professional life are entirely abandoned'. This is a real possibility. In at least one case the parishioners of one of the dossier's priests publicly demanded that he be reinstated. In a nutshell, this stance views clerical double lives – priests not practising what they preach – benevolently, seeing them as victims of an overly rigid system or at least one which asks just a little too much of them, imposing impossible rules on them. It is this which is behind the understanding and respect for the professional and human qualities of cheating priests.

The fact is that, for those who reason in this way, the spiritual and moral benefits of the work of a good priest are such as to merit turning a blind eye to their private behaviour, to what are generously described as dalliances, or as venial sins, if priests perform their pastoral duties conscientiously. It is reasoning similar to that of those who so enjoy the Pope's speeches on the importance of poverty or gestures such as that of his almoner, involving reconnecting the electricity at a refugee shelter, but who ignore the fact that the assets of the Catholic Church (made up of many thousands of movable and immovable properties, universities, schools, hospitals, etc.) have been valued at over 2,000 billion Euros and are managed by criteria identical to those of organisations all over the world.

My own opinion is that there is at least one positive outcome of this approach: acceptance of the fact that priests are, in the last analysis, entirely normal people with the same needs and reactions as everyone else. No ontological transformation has made them capable of repressing their desires and making them more like angels. My research might help this vast group of people 'indifferent' to clerical celibacy to pay more careful attention to the sufferings of those who end up living decades of lonely double lives, tragically marked by lies and non-authenticity, and are encouraged to do so by the institution they belong to.

In any event, alongside what I have described here, there is one social group (by no means negligible in size) which cannot ignore the accounts in this book. This is made up of all those people who – whether they like it or not – have suffered violence and abuse by members of the clergy. I am not talking about children alone, but also nuns, lay women, and adult seminarians.[1] Those committing such violence are undoubtedly individually responsible for their actions and where crimes are concerned it is right that they should be sent to prison. The laws of certain countries, including France's, also condemn the ecclesiastical authorities who ignore the huge suffering of the victims and help abusers escape punishment, covering up, protecting and looking after them.[2] What the courts can do nothing about, however – because it falls outside the sphere of personal responsibility – is the clerical culture described in this book, the breeding ground of these abuses and violence. If this culture did not exist or was less powerful it would be impossible for abusing priests to convince their victims to submit on the grounds that 'it is God's will', 'because priests know better than anyone what can and can't be done, what is right and what is wrong'. In other words, without clerical culture victims' docility, i.e. the fact that a lot of people place blind trust in men held to be morally and spiritually superior and believe them to be incapable of harm, would be difficult to explain. Without the celibacy rule and the customary silence and hypocrisy around everything to do with sex learnt in many years at the seminary, profound sexual immaturity, delayed adulthood and sexual abuses would be less widespread in the priesthood.

Without the training ground in abuse constituted by the seminaries some priests would do less harm in the world. Without the encouragement they receive to consider sex as simply a distressing need, priests would be better able to identify their own feelings and emotional needs and those of others. Without the nightmare of secrecy and scandals, without the fixation with sex as mere bestial satisfaction of personal urges, without their belief in their right to everything and duty to nothing and no-one, of being held to account only to their superiors and never to the vulnerable, priests might find it easier to acknowledge other people's existence, and that sex has psychological and emotional consequences for oneself and one's partner and is not simply a matter of 'scratching an itch' as quickly as possible and without being found out. If priests were not totally dependent on the institution they would not see themselves as free to get up to anything because the Holy Mother Church will get them out of any trouble. And we could go on but it would be the beginning of a new, yet to be written, book. The mountain is high but the climb has begun.

Notes

1 The issue has been discussed but above all in English. I have already and repeatedly cited Keenan's excellent research (2013). See also excellent work by Frawley-O'Dea (2007 and 2009), Sipe (1995) and edited by Doyle, Sipe and Wall (2006), as well as articles by Celenza (2005), Doyle (2003) and Lüdecke (2010). For a more general overview of the paedophilia theme, see Schinaia (2010).
2 This comes across clearly from the six-month suspended prison sentence given to the Archbishop of Lyon and Head of the French Church Cardinal Barbarin, held to be guilty of covering up the sex crimes of Bernard Preynat.

References

Anderson, J. (2005). *Priests in Love: Roman Catholic Clergy and Their Intimate Relationships*, London: Continuum.
Badaracchi, L. (2009). *Fare il prete non è un mestiere. Una vocazione alla prova*, Roma: Edizioni dell'Asino.
Bèraud, C. (2006). *Le Métier de prêtre. Approche sociologique*, Paris: Éditions de l'Atelier.
Brunsson, N. (1989). *The Organization of Hypocrisy: Talk, Decisions and Actions in Organizations*, New York: John Wiley & Sons.
Cardano, M. (2011). *La ricerca qualitativa*, Bologna: il Mulino.
Castegnaro, A. (2006). *Preti del Nordest*, Venezia: Marcianum Press.
Castegnaro, A. (2010). 'Ridare forma al presbiterio. Fare il prete: disagio e trasformazione', in *Il Regno-Attualità*, 12, pp. 414–421.
Castegnaro, A. (2018). 'Ci sarà un parroco nel nostro futuro? Il parroco oggi. Uno sguardo sociologico', in *Credere Oggi*, 225, pp. 9–34.
Catechism of the Catholic Church. (2016). *Catechism of the Catholic Church* (2nd edn), Washington, DC: United States Conference of Catholic Bishops.
Catino, M. (2023). *Scapegoating: How Organizations Assign Blame*. Cambridge, Cambridge University Press.
Celenza, A. (2005). 'Sexual Misconduct in the Clergy: The Search for the Father', in *Studies in Gender & Sexuality*, 5, pp. 213–232.
Clegg, S. R., Courpasson, D., & Phillips N. (2006). *Power and Organizations*, London: Sage.
Cohen, S. (2013). *States of Denial: Knowing About Atrocities and Suffering*, New York: John Wiley & Sons.
Congregation for the Clergy. (2016). *The Gift of the Priestly Vocation*, Vatican City: Dicastery for the Clergy.
Cozzens, D. B. (2000). *The Changing Face of the Priesthood: A Reflection on the Priest's Crisis of Soul*, Collegeville, MN: Liturgical Press.
Cozzens, D. B. (2004) *Sacred Silence: Denial and the Crisis in the Church*, Collegeville, MN: Liturgical Press.
Cozzens, D. B. (2006) *Freeing Celibacy*, Collegeville, MN: Liturgical Press.
Crea, G. (2015). *Tonache ferite. Forme del disagio nella vita religiosa e sacerdotale*, Bologna: EDB.
Crea, G., & Mastrofini, F. (2010). *Preti sul lettino*, Firenze: Giunti.
Dalla Zuanna, G., & Ronzoni, G. (2003). *Meno preti, quale chiesa? Per non abbandonare le parrocchie*, Bologna: EDB.

References

Dinter, P. E. (2003). *The Other Side of the Altar: One Man's Life in the Catholic Priesthood*, New York: Farrar, Straus and Giroux.

Diotallevi, L. (2017). *Fine corsa: la crisi del cristianesimo come religione confessionale*, Bologna: EDB.

Dos Santos, E. A., & Guareschi, P. A. (2019). 'Rappresentazioni sociali dell'omosessualità', in *Il Regno-Documenti*, 7, pp. 248–256.

Doyle, T. P. (2003). 'Roman Catholic Clericalism, Religious Duress, and Clergy Sexual Abuse', in *Pastoral Psychology*, 51, 3, pp. 189–231.

Doyle, T. P., Sipe, A. W. R., & Wall, P. J. (2006). *Sex, Priests, and Secret Codes: The Catholic Church's 2000-Year Paper Trail of Sexual Abuse*, Los Angeles, CA: Volt Press.

Drewermann, E. (1995). *Funzionari di Dio: psicogramma di un ideale*, Bolzano: Rætia.

Foucault, M. (2007). *Security, Territory, Population: Lectures at the Collège de France 1977–1978*, London: Palgrave Macmillan.

Foucault, M. (2010). *The Government of Self and Others: Lectures at the Collège de France 1982–1983*, London: Palgrave Macmillan.

Foucault, M. (2011). *The Courage of Truth: Lectures at the Collège de France 1983–1984*, London: Palgrave Macmillan.

Foucault, Michel (2020). *The History of Sexuality: The Will to Knowledge*, London: Penguin Classics.

Foucault, M. (2024). *The Japan Lectures. A Transational Critical Encounter*, London: Routledge.

Frawley-O'Dea, M. G. (2007). *Perversion of Power: Sexual Abuse in the Catholic Church*, Nashville, TN: Vanderbilt University Press.

Frawley-O'Dea, M. G., & Goldner, V. (eds) (2007). *Predatory Priests, Silenced Victims. The Sexual Abuse Crisis and the Catholic Church*, London: The Analytic Press.

Frings, T. (2018). *Così non posso più fare il parroco. Vi racconto perché*, Roma: Ancora.

Geertz, C. (1973). *The Interpretation of Cultures*, New York: Basic Books.

Glaser, B. G., & Strauss, A. L. (1965). *Awareness Of Dying*, Chicago, IL: Aldine Publishing Company.

Goffman, E. (1961). *Asylums: Essays on the Social Situation of Mental Patients and Other Inmates*, New York: Doubleday Anchor.

Hammersley, M., & Atkinson, P. (2019). *Ethnography: Principles in Practice*, London: Routledge.

Hannan, M. T., & Freeman, J. (1984). 'Structural Inertia and Organizational Change', in *American Sociological Review*, 49, 2, pp. 149–164.

Hannan, M. T. & Freeman, J. (1989). *Organizational Ecology*, Cambridge, MA: Harvard University Press.

Hoge, D. R. (2005). *Center of Catholic Identity*, Available at http://bit.ly/2TkOKQF.

Hoge, D. R., Potvin, R. H., & Ferry, Kathleen M. (1984) *Research on Men's Vocations to the Priesthood and the Religious Life*, United States Catholic Conference.

Hoge, D. R., & Wenger, J. E. (2003) *Evolving Visions of the Priesthood: Changes from Vatican II to the Turn of the New Century*, Collegeville, MN: Liturgical Press.

Jordan, M. D. (2000). *The Silence of Sodom: Homosexuality in Modern Catholicism*, Chicago: University of Chicago Press.

Kappler, S., Hancock, K. A., & Plante, T. G. (2013). 'Roman Catholic Gay Priests: Internalized Homophobia, Sexual Identity, and Psychological Well-Being', in *Pastoral Psychology*, 62, 6, pp. 805–826.

Keenan, M. (2012). *Child Sexual Abuse and the Catholic Church: Gender, Power, and Organizational Culture*, Oxford: Oxford University Press.

Kinsey, A. C. (1998). *Sexual Behaviour in the Human Male*, Bloomington, IN: Indiana University Press.

Kochansky, G. E., & Cohen, M. L. (2007). 'Priests Who Sexualize Minors: Psychodynamic, Characterological, and Clerical Considerations' in Frawley-O' Dea M. G. and Goldner V. (eds), *Predatory Priests, Silenced Victims. The Sexual Abuse Crisis and the Catholic Church*, London: The Analytic Press, pp. 35–57.

Kueffler, M. (2011) 'La rinuncia sessuale e la modernità', in *Contemporanea*, 14, 4, pp. 704–710.

Laqueur, T. W. (2003). *Solitary Sex: A Cultural History of Masturbation*, New York: Zone Books.

Lüdecke, N. (2010) 'Le violenze di preti su minori nel diritto canonico', in *Il Regno-Documenti*, 55, pp. 470–483.

Lukes, S. (2021). *Power: A Radical View*, London: Bloomsbury Publishing.

Martel, F. (2019). *In the Closet of the Vatican: Power, Homosexuality, Hypocrisy*. London: Bloomsbury Continuum.

Marzano, M. (2004). *Scene finali*, Bologna: il Mulino.

Marzano, M. (2006). *Etnografia e ricerca sociale*, Roma-Bari: Laterza.

Marzano, M. (2009). *Cattolicesimo magico*, Milano:Bompiani.

Marzano, M. (2012). *Quel che resta dei cattolici*, Milano:Feltrinelli.

Marzano, M. (2018). *La chiesa immobile*, Roma-Bari: Laterza.

Maslow, A. H. (1970). *Motivation and Personality* (2nd edn.). New York: Harper and Row.

McGlone, G. J. (2002) *Sexually Offending and Non-offending Roman Catholic Priests: Characterization and Analysis*, Unpublished Dissertation, California School of Professional Psychology, San Diego.

Morrison, E. W., & Milliken, F. J. (2000) 'Organizational Silence: A Barrier to Change and Development in a Pluralistic World', in *Academy of Management Review*, 25, 4, pp. 706–725.

Pope Francis (2018). *The Strength of a Vocation: Consecrated Life Today*, Washington, DC: United States Conference of Catholic Bishops.

Papesh, M. L. (2004). *Clerical Culture: Contradiction and Transformation: The Culture of the Diocesan Priests of the United States Catholic Church*, Collegeville, MN: Liturgical Press.

Pesce, M. (2009). 'Introduzione all'edizione italiana' in Frawley-O'Dea, M. G., & Goldner, V. (eds), *Atti impuri: la piaga dell'abuso sessuale nella Chiesa cattolica*, Milano, Cortina, pp. XV–XXI.

Petrà, B. (2011). *Preti celibi e preti sposati. Due carismi della Chiesa cattolica*, Assisi: Cittadella Editrice.

Politi, M. (2000). *La confessione. Un prete gay racconta la sua storia*, Roma: Editori Riuniti.

Portier, P. (2012). 'Pluralité et unité dans le catholicisme français', in Béraud, C., Gugelot, F. & Saint-Martin, I., *Catholicisme en tensions*, Paris, Éditions de l'Ehess, pp. 19–36.

Phipps, W. E. (2004). *Clerical Celibacy: The Heritage*, New York: Continuum.

Qirko, N.H. (2001.) 'The Maintenance and Reinforcement of Celibacy in Institutionalized Settings', in Sobo, E. J. & Bell, S., *Celibacy, Culture, and Society: The Anthropology of Sexual Abstinence*, Madison, WI: University of Wisconsin Press, pp. 65–87.

References

Robinson, G. (2008). *Confronting Power and Sex in the Catholic Church: Reclaiming the Spirit of Jesus*, Collegeville, MN: Liturgical Press.

Ronzoni, G. (ed.) (2008). *Ardere, non bruciarsi. Studio sul 'burnout' tra il clero diocesano*, Padova: Edizioni Messaggero.

Schein, E. H. (2010). *Organizational Culture and Leadership*. New York: John Wiley & Sons.

Schinaia, C. (2010). *On Paedophilia*, London: Routledge.

Schlegel, J. (2013). 'Qu'est-ce que le 'lobby gay' du Vatican?', in *Fait religieux*, 20, giugno.

Schlüsser-Florenza, E. (1983). *In Memory of Her. A Feminist Theological Reconstruction of Christian Origins*, London: SCM Press.

Schoenherr, R.A. (2004). *Goodbye Father: The Celibate Male Priesthood and the Future of the Catholic Church*, Oxford: Oxford University Press.

Selznick, P. (2011). *Leadership in Administration: A Sociological Interpretation*, New Orleans: Quid Pro Books.

Semeraro, M. (2018). *Preti senza battesimo? Una provocazione, non un giudizio*, Cinisello Balsamo: San Paolo Edizioni.

Simmel, G. (1906). 'The Sociology of Secrecy and of Secret Societies'. *American Journal of Sociology*, 11, 4, pp. 441–498.

Sipe, A. W. R. (1995). *Sex, Priests, and Power: Anatomy of a Crisis*, London: Psychology Press.

Sipe, A. W. R. (2003). *Celibacy In Crisis: A Secret World Revisited*, London: Routledge.

Sipe, A. W. R. (2013). *A Secret World: Sexuality and the Search for Celibacy*, London: Routledge.

Sobo, E. J., & Bell, S. (eds) (2001). *Celibacy, Culture, and Society: The Anthropology of Sexual Abstinence*, Madison, WI: University of Wisconsin Press.

Stengers J., & Van Neck, A. (2001). *Masturbation: The History of the Great Terror*, New York: Palgrave, 2001.

Stinchcombe, A.L. (2000). 'Social Structure and Organizations', in Dobbin, F. & Baum, J. A. C. (eds), *Economics Meets Sociology in Strategic Management*, Leeds: Emerald Group Publishing Limited, pp. 229–259.

Stuart, E. (1993). *Chosen: Gay Catholic Priests Tell Their Stories*, London: Geoffrey Chapman.

Tricou, J. (2018). 'The Remaking of "Moles". Governing Gay Priests' Silence at the Time of Gay Marriage', in *Sociologie*, 9, 2, pp. 131–150.

Turina, I. (2013). *Chiesa e biopolitica: il discorso cattolico su famiglia, sessualità e vita umana da Pio XI a Benedetto XVI*, Sesto San Giovanni: Mimesis.

VV.AA. (2008) *Preti sposati nella chiesa cattolica*, Molfetta (Bari): La Meridiana.

Walker, G. (2007). *Celibacy and Misogyny*, in Frawley-O' Dea, M. G. and Goldner, V. (eds), *Predatory Priests, Silenced Victims: The Sexual Abuse Crisis and the Catholic Church*, London: The Analytic Press, pp. 213–230.

Wagner, R. 1981 *Gay Catholic Priests: A Study of Cognitive and Affective Dissonance*, San Francisco, CA: Specific Press.

Weber, M. (1978). *Economy and Society: An Outline of Interpretive Sociology*, Berkeley, CA: University of California Press.

Wilson, G. B. (2008). *Clericalism: The Death of Priesthood*, Collegeville, MN: Liturgical Press.

Wolf, H. (2019). *Contro il celibato*, Roma: Donzelli.

Wolf, J. G. (1989). *Gay Priests*, San Francisco, CA: Harper and Row.

Zerubavel, E. (2006). *The Elephant in the Room: Silence and Denial in Everyday Life*, Oxford: Oxford University Press.

Index

Anderson 86

Badaracchi 13n
Barbarin 106n
Béraud 38

Calvin 60
Canon Law 20
Castegnaro 13n
Catechism of the Catholic Church 15, 51, 55
Catino 10
Celenza 43, 106n
Clegg 12
Cohen M.L. 39, 43
Cohen S. 12
Congregation for Catholic Education 55
Congregation for the Clergy 54n
Courpasson 12
Cozzens 12, 21, 23, 39, 58
Crea 13n

Dalla Zuanna 13n
Dinter 43
Diotallevi 101
Dos Santos 71, 72
Doyle 106n
Drewermann 21, 45, 52, 63

Ferry 39
FIDES 19n, 31n.
Foucault 13, 17–18, 23, 101
Francis Pope 25, 56, 60n
Frawley-O'Dea 21, 39, 43, 106n
Freeman 14
Frings 13n
Fuchs 48

Geertz 12
Glaser 84
Goffman 28, 32, 45–46, 50, 86
Guareschi 71, 72

Hancock 60
Hannan 14
Hoge 39, 43, 60

Jordan 22, 26, 40, 50, 52, 57–60n, 73, 82

Kappler 60
Keenan 32, 48, 50, 52, 106n
Kinsey 52, 54n
Kochansky 39, 43
Kueffler 23, 24

Laqueur 54
Lepore 62, 63
Lüdecke 15, 16, 106n
Lukes 12
Luther 60

Mangiacapra 96–98, 100, 104
Martel 58, 59, 62, 67, 99
Marzano 6, 8, 12–14, 27
Maslow 23
Masters 52
Mastrofini 13n
McGlone 87
Milliken 12
Morrison 12

Orwell 84

Pallavicini (cardinal) 26
Pesce 18, 19
Petrà 26n
Pew Research Center 23

Phillips 12
Phipps 60
Plante 60
Portier 38
Potvin 39
Preynat 106n

Qirko 60

Ronzoni 13n

Schein 74
Schinaia 106n
Schlegel 72
Schlüsser-Florenza 39
Selznick 14
Semeraro 13n, 26n
Simmel 12
Sipe 39–41, 51–52, 60, 73, 82, 86, 104, 106n
Stengers 54

Stinchcombe 14
Strauss 84

Tricou 38, 48, 57, 59, 63, 68, 72
Turina 60n

Univision 22

Van Necl 54
Viganò 60n
VV.AA. 26n

Wagner 52, 54n, 60
Walker 39, 40
Wall 106n
Weber 16, 20, 22–23
Wenger 60
Wolf H. 21, 23, 24, 26n
Wolf J.G. 59

Zerubavel 12, 83, 84